Geopolitics

Geopolitics

From the Cold War
to the 21st Century

Francis P. Sempa

Transaction Publishers
New Brunswick (U.S.A.) and London (U.K.)

First paperback printing 2007
Copyright © 1989 by Transaction Publishers, New Brunswick, New Jersey.

This book is printed on acid-free paper that meets the American National Standard for Permanence of Paper for Printed Library Materials.

Library of Congress Catalog Number: 2002020454
ISBN: 978-0-7658-0122-7 (cloth); 978-1-4128-0726-5 (paper)
Printed in the United States of America

Library of Congress Cataloging-in-Publication Data

Sempa, Francis P.
    Geopolitics : from the Cold War to the 21st century / Francis P. Sempa.
        p. cm.
    Includes bibliographical references and index.
    ISBN 0-7658-0122-1 (alk. paper)
    1. Geopolitics. 2. Cold War. 3. Post-communism. I. Title.

JC319.S45 2002
320.1'2—dc21   2002020454

"To the memory of my father, Frank P. Sempa,
journalist, editor, patriot,
and soldier of the greatest generation."

Contents

Acknowledgements

"Mackinder's World," first appeared in the Winter 2000 issue of *American Diplomacy* (*www.americandiplomacy.com*).

"The Geopolitics Man," first appeared in slightly different form in the Fall 1992 issue of *The National Interest*.

"The First Cold Warrior," first appeared in the Fall 2000 issue of *American Diplomacy*.

"Geopolitics and American Strategy in the Cold War," first appeared in slightly different form in the Spring 1987 issue of *Strategic Review*.

"The Geopolitics of the Post-Cold War World," appeared in slightly different form in the Winter 1992 issue of *Strategic Review*.

"Why Teach Geopolitics?," appeared in slightly different form in the Winter 1990 issue of the *International Social Science Review*.

Part 1

Geopolitical Perspectives

1

Introduction: The Geopolitics of History

"Geopolitics" is a much-overused term. Writers, observers, and practitioners of international politics frequently invoke the term to describe, explain, or analyze specific foreign policy issues and problems. Such overuse ignores the fact that geopolitics as a method of analyzing international relations has a history that includes a common vocabulary, well-established if sometimes conflicting concepts, an established body of thought, and a recognized group of theorists and scholars.

The goal of this book is to present salient aspects of the history of geopolitical thought and to apply classical geopolitical analysis to past, recent, and current international relations. Pride of place is given to the geopolitical ideas and theories of Halford Mackinder, Alfred Thayer Mahan, Nicholas Spykman, and James Burnham. These "geopoliticians" combined brilliant analyses of past events with remarkable predictions of future developments. Mackinder, for example, foresaw in the early 1920s, and again in 1943, the emergence of the North Atlantic Alliance that was founded in 1949. Burnham in the late 1940s and early 1950s proposed a strategy to undermine Soviet power in Central and Eastern Europe that foreshadowed the successful policies of the Reagan administration in the 1980s.

The end of the Cold War resulted in hopes for a "new world order" and predictions that economics, or as Edward Luttwak put it, "geo-economics," would replace geopolitics as the driving force in international politics. Events soon proved that geography still matters; that nations still struggle for power and territory; that military power still trumps economics (at least in the short run); that we are not, contrary to Francis Fukuyama, at "the end of history."

The Cold War was not the end of history, but rather the most recent collision between a potentially hegemonic power and a coalition of states opposed to that power's bid for global hegemony. Before the Soviet Union, there was Hitler's Germany allied to Imperial Japan. Before Hitler's Germany and Japan there was Wilhelm II's Germany and Austria-Hungary. Before Germany and Austria-Hungary there was Napoleon's France. Before Napoleon there was the France of Louis XIV. Before Louis XIV there was the Austrian and Spanish Hapsburgs. Each bid for hegemony was countered by a coalition of states determined to reestablish or uphold the balance of power.

There is no reason to believe that the twenty-first century will be any different. There are unmistakable signs that China is in the early stages of a bid to become the dominant power in the Asia-Pacific region and beyond. This is a potential threat that the United States ignores at its peril. With Russia currently undergoing another "time of troubles," and Europe dominated by peaceful democracies, the world's focus has shifted to Central Asia, Southwest Asia, East Asia, and the Pacific Rim. Due to many factors, including the break-up of the Soviet Empire, large supplies of oil and natural gas in the Caspian Sea region, the nuclear dimension to the India-Pakistan conflict, and the rise of China, this huge region has once again become what Alfred Thayer Mahan called the "debatable and debated ground." Russia, Turkey, Iran, India, Pakistan, China, Japan, the Koreas and the United States have interests that collide in one or more areas of this region.

Previous global or regional power struggles involved battles on land, at sea, and in the air. The twenty-first century's struggles will likely involve efforts to gain control of outer space or at least to deny to others the use of outer space. Anti-satellite weapons, space-based lasers, ballistic missile defenses, and orbital space stations are no longer the stuff of science fiction. The impact of technology will force statesmen to enlarge their geopolitical vision.

Geopolitics is about perspective. It is about how one views the world. In elementary and high school geography classes, we were taught that the world is composed of seven continents (Europe, Asia, Africa, North America, South America, Australia, and Antarctica) and four oceans (Atlantic, Pacific, Indian, and Arctic). Viewed geopolitically, however, the world is composed of one great continent, Eurasia-Africa, many smaller islands, and one great ocean. This distinction between geography and geopolitics is important to the study and practice of international relations.

Knowledge of geography is essential to geopolitical analysis. Geopolitics is about the interaction among states and empires in a particular geographical setting. Throughout history, geography has been the stage on which nations and empires have collided. Geography is the most fundamental factor in international politics because it is the most permanent. The geography of a state—its position in a geographical region and in the world as a whole—presents opportunities to, and imposes limitations on, the state. For that reason, geography also conditions the perspectives of a state's leaders or rulers and, thereby, affects their decision-making in matters of foreign policy.

Throughout history, geography has influenced the geopolitical orientation of countries in the direction of either land power or sea power. An insular or island location will likely orient a country to the sea, whereas a continental location will likely orient a country toward land. Some countries are located on continents but have ready access to the ocean, a situation that can result in a sea or land orientation. The sea or land orientation of a country is not necessarily absolute. A sea-oriented country may be able to project power on land, and a land-oriented country may take to the sea. When that happens, as when Wilhelmine Germany sought to challenge British sea power in the early 1900s, conflict often ensues.

The sheer size of a country is an important factor in the role it can play in international politics. In recent times, the dominant geopolitical players were the Soviet Union and the United States, two continental-sized giants. But the size of a country alone is insufficient to guarantee geopolitical significance. Brazil, Argentina, and Australia are large countries that, by themselves, have never played a significant role in world politics. The much smaller countries of England and Japan, meanwhile, have ruled great empires.

Geographical position—where a country is located relative to other countries—is more important than size. The study of world history shows, for example, that countries located wholly or mostly in the Northern Hemisphere have had the greatest impact on world politics. Until the twentieth century, world politics was dominated by countries located on Eurasia, its offshore islands, and Africa, north of the Sahara. For many centuries, the Western and Southern Hemispheres were little more than the objects of Eurasian colonial powers. The United States is the only Western Hemispheric country to greatly impact global politics.

Other factors that affect a country's ability to play a significant role on the world stage include population, economics, technology, military power, and character of government. Those factors, however, unlike geography, are subject to change over time. Geography is constant, though its impact can change. Technological and scientific advances can alter the effects of distance, topography, and climate. The protection afforded the United States by the Atlantic and Pacific Oceans, for example, has lessened over time with the development of faster ships and submarines, airplanes and jets, and intercontinental ballistic missiles.

At its most fundamental level, international politics is about the struggle for space and power. Throughout history, nations and empires have sought to expand their territory and their influence over other countries and peoples. History records the rise and fall of empires and whole civilizations, most compellingly catalogued by Arnold J. Toynbee in his twelve-volume *A Study of History*. Toynbee argued that civilizations rise and fall due to the dialectic of "challenge and response." In international politics, challenges have frequently taken the form of rising powers that upset or threaten to upset the existing balance of power. After the Napoleonic Wars, the diplomacy of the Congress of Vienna resulted in what Henry Kissinger called "a world restored"—an international structure or system that lasted until the First World War. The challenge to the "structure of peace" established by the Congress of Vienna emerged in 1871 with the rise of Germany to a dominant position in the center of Europe. Today, the international system created by the end of the Cold War is being challenged by the rise of China in the East Asia-Pacific Rim region.

The United States, meanwhile, has emerged as the geopolitical successor to the British Empire. In the nineteenth century, Britain used its insular geographical position and command of the seas to support the European balance of power erected at the Congress of Vienna. Today, the United States uses its insular geographical position and command of the sea, air and space to support the Eurasian balance of power in the wake of the Cold War.

Lord Palmerston famously remarked that nations have no permanent friends and no permanent enemies, only permanent interests. Geopolitics helps statesmen determine their country's interests, and helps them distinguish between enduring and transient interests. Those interests can, of course, change over time. In the sixteenth and seventeenth centuries, for example, England sought to prevent a hostile power from controlling Belgium. Later, as her empire expanded, England sought to maintain command of the seas and an evenly balanced European continent. Finally, as her empire faded, England supported a strong NATO and a "special relationship" with the United States.

U.S. foreign policy had a similar evolution. Initially, after the War of Independence, the United States sought to eliminate European influence on the American continent and to expand westward (the Monroe Doctrine and Manifest Destiny). In the late nineteenth century, the United States sought to expand into the Pacific Ocean and East Asia (the Open Door). In the twentieth century, the centerpiece of U.S. foreign policy was to prevent a hostile power or alliance of powers from dominating Europe or East Asia (containment).

The geopolitics of the twenty-first century is taking shape. Globalization, economic interdependence, and the information revolution will affect how nations interact in this century. But those factors have not rendered geopolitics irrelevant. Instead, those factors and others will operate on nations within a larger geopolitical framework. To understand where we are, however, it is necessary to look back into the geopolitics of history. To do that, we need to familiarize ourselves with the timeless methods of geopolitical analysis employed by the great geopolitical theorists.

In other words, we need to see the world as Mackinder, Mahan, Spykman, and Burnham saw it.

2

Mackinder's World

The study of international relations is impossible without a firm grasp of geography. The geographic factor in world history is the most fundamental because it is the most constant. Populations increase and decrease, natural resources are discovered and expended, political systems frequently change, empires and states rise and fall, technologies decline and advance, but the location of continents, islands, seas, and oceans has not changed significantly throughout recorded history. That is why great nations neglect the study of geography at their peril.

No one understood better the important relationship between geography and world history than the great British geographer, Halford John Mackinder. Born in Gainsborough, England in 1861, Mackinder attended Gainsborough Grammar School and Epsom College before entering Oxford in 1880. As a boy, according to W. H. Parker, Mackinder had "a strong curiosity about natural phenomena,... a love of the history of travel and exploration, an interest in international affairs, and a passion for making maps."[1]

At Oxford, Mackinder fell under the influence of Michael Sadler and Henry Nottidge Mosely, key figures in the effort to establish geography as an independent field of study in England. Mackinder was appointed a lecturer in natural science and economic history in 1886 and that same year joined the Royal Geographical Society. According to Brian W. Blouet, one of Mackinder's biographers, the membership of the Royal Geographical Society "consisted of men with a general interest in the world and its affairs, officers from the army and navy, businessmen, academics, schoolteachers, diplomats, and colonial administrators."[2] The next year (1887), Mackinder wrote his first major paper, "On the Scope and Methods of Geography," which has been called "a classic document in the history of the development of British geography."[3] In that paper, Mackinder argued that "rational" political geography was "built upon and subsequent to physical geography." "Everywhere," he wrote, "political questions will depend on the results of the physical inquiry." Political geography's function was "to trace the interaction between man and his environment." That environment, Mackinder explained, included the "configuration of the earth's surface," climate and weather conditions, and the presence or absence of natural resources.[4]

Four of the ideas mentioned in "On the Scope and Methods of Geography" are key to understanding Mackinder's subsequent geopolitical writings. First, Mackinder expressed his view that the goal of a geographer was to "look at the past [so] that he may interpret the present." Second, he noted that man's great geographical discoveries were nearing an end; there were very few "blanks remaining on our maps." Third, Mackinder described the two kinds of political conquerors as "land-wolves and sea-wolves." And, fourth, he recognized that technological improvements made possible "the great size of modern states."[5] Upon the foundation of those four ideas Mackinder later constructed his famous global theory.

In June 1887, Mackinder was appointed Reader in Geography at Oxford, and he began to lecture on the influence of geography on European history. He visited the United States in 1892, lecturing at the University of Pennsylvania, Swarthmore, Drexel, Harvard, Princeton, and Johns Hopkins. The same year, he was appointed Principal of Reading College at Oxford, a position he held for eleven years. In 1893-1894, Mackinder gave a series of ten lectures on the relations of geography to history in Europe and Asia. Five years later, he helped found the School of Geography at Oxford, and participated in an expedition that climbed Mt. Kenya, Africa's second-highest peak.[6]

In 1902, Mackinder wrote his first major book, *Britain and the British Seas*. Although primarily concerned, in Mackinder's words, "to present a picture of the physical features and conditions" of Britain,[7] the book's chapters on "The Position of Britain," "Strategic Geography," and "Imperial Britain" contain insights on global affairs that foreshadowed Mackinder's subsequent geopolitical works. In the book, he described Britain as being "of Europe, yet not in Europe," and as lying "off the shores of the great continent."[8] British predominance in the world rested on its "command of the sea," wrote Mackinder, because "[t]he unity of the ocean is the simple physical fact underlying the dominant value of sea-power in the modern globe-wide world."[9] "A new balance of power is being evolved," Mackinder opined, and it included "five great world states, Britain, France, Germany, Russia, and America."[10] Mackinder suggested, however, that Britain's position as the preeminent world power was endangered due to "permanent facts of physical geography" in the form of "the presence of vast Powers, broad-based on the resources of half continents" (that is Russia and the United States).[11]

The threat to British preeminence and to the liberty of the world was the subject of Mackinder's bold, provocative essay, "The Geographical Pivot of History," which he delivered to the Royal Geographical Society on January 25, 1904. He began this seminal work by noting that the last stage of "geographical exploration" (which he called the "Columbian epoch") was nearing its end. "In 400 years," he wrote, "the outline of the map of the world has been completed with approximate accuracy."[12] Moreover, since conquerors, missionaries, miners, farmers, and engineers "followed so closely in the travelers' footsteps," the world was for the first time a "closed political system."[13] This meant, wrote Mackinder, that "every explosion of social forces, instead of being dissipated in a surrounding circuit of unknown space and barbaric chaos, will be sharply re-echoed from the far side of the globe, and weak elements in the political and economic organism of the world will be shattered in consequence."[14] Nations, in other words, could no longer safely ignore major events that occurred in far away places of the globe.

Mackinder's avowed purposes in writing the "pivot" paper were to establish "a correlation between the larger geographical and the larger historical generalizations," to provide "a formula which shall express certain aspects... of geographical causation in universal history," and to set "into perspective some of the competing forces in current international politics."[15]

Mackinder pictured Europe and Asia as one great continent: "Euro-Asia." He described Euro-Asia as "a continuous land, ice-girt in the north, water-girt elsewhere, measuring twenty-one million square miles." The center and north of Euro-Asia, he pointed out, measure "some nine million square miles,... have no available waterways to the ocean, but, on the other hand,... are generally favorable to the mobility of horsemen." To the "east and south of this heart-land," he further explained, "are marginal regions, ranged in a vast crescent, accessible to shipmen."[16]

Mackinder noted that between the fifth and sixteenth centuries, a "succession of ... nomadic peoples" (Huns, Avars, Bulgarians, Magyars, Khazars, Patzinaks, Cumans, Mongols, and Kalmuks) emerged from Central Asia to conquer or threaten the states and peoples located in the "marginal crescent" (Europe, the Middle East, Southwest Asia, China, Southeast Asia, Korea, and Japan). Beginning in the late fifteenth century, however, the "great mariners of the Columbian generation" used sea power to envelop Central Asia. "The broad political effect" of the rise of sea powers, explained Mackinder, "was to reverse the relations of Europe and Asia." "[W]hereas in the Middle Ages Europe was caged between an impassable desert to south, an unknown ocean to west, and icy or forested wastes to north and north-east, and in the east and south-east was constantly threatened by the superior mobility of the horsemen," Mackinder further explained, " she now emerged upon the world, multiplying more than thirty-fold the sea surface and coastal lands to which she had access, and wrapping her influence around the Euro-Asiatic land-power which had hitherto threatened her very existence."[17]

Often unappreciated, however, Mackinder believed, was the fact that while Europe expanded overseas, the Russian state, based in Eastern Europe and Central Asia, expanded to the south and east, organizing a vast space of great human and natural resources. That vast space would soon be "covered with a network of railways," thereby greatly enhancing the mobility and strategic reach of land power. [18]

With that geo historical background, Mackinder identified the northern-central core of Euro-Asia as the "pivot region" or "pivot state" of world politics. He placed Germany, Austria, Turkey, India, and China, lands immediately adjacent to the pivot region, in an "inner crescent," and the insular nations of Britain, South Africa, Australia, the United States, Canada, and Japan in an "outer crescent." He then warned that, "[t]he oversetting of the balance of power in favour of the pivot state, resulting in its expansion over the marginal lands of Euro-Asia, would permit the use of vast continental resources for fleet-building, and the empire of the world would then be in sight."[19] Mackinder suggested that either a Russo-German alliance or a Sino-Japanese empire (which conquered Russian territory) could contend for world hegemony. In either case, "oceanic frontage" would be added to "the resources of the great continent," thereby creating the geopolitical conditions necessary for producing a great power that was supreme both on land and at sea.[20]

"I have spoken as a geographer," Mackinder acknowledged toward the end of the paper. But he carefully avoided geographical determinism in assessing the world situation: "The actual balance of political power at any given time is... the product, on the one hand, of geographical conditions, both economic and strategic, and, on the other hand, of the relative number, virility, equipment and organization of the competing peoples."[21]

Mackinder's "pivot" paper caused one member of the Royal Geographical Society to "look with regret on some of the space which is unoccupied here."[22] Unfortunately, as W. H. Parker has pointed out, "in the English-speaking world Mackinder's paper lay forgotten... for thirty-five years."[23] It was only during and after the Second World War that Englishmen and Americans began to appreciate the wisdom and prescience of Mackinder's "pivot" paper and his 1919 masterpiece, *Democratic Ideals and Reality*.

A few months before he delivered the "pivot" paper to the Royal Geographical Society, Mackinder was appointed the director of the London School of Economics, a post that he held until 1908. In 1910 he was elected to the House of Commons, where he served until 1922. In 1919, as civil war raged in Russia, Lord Curzon, the Foreign Secretary, chose Mackinder to be British High Commissioner for South Russia. In that post, Mackinder promoted the idea of a British-supported anti-Bolshevik alliance because he feared that if the Bolsheviks consolidated their control of Russia "there is... great risk that such a weapon may be forged as may become a danger to the world." "[T]here is to-day," he warned, "a growing threat from Moscow of a state of affairs which will render this world a very unsafe place for democracies."[24] Among British policymakers of the time, only Winston Churchill voiced strong support for Mackinder's anti-Bolshevik strategy.

During his directorship of the London School of Economics and his stay in Parliament, Mackinder continued to think and write on geography and world affairs. His articles and books included: "Man-Power as a Measure of National and Imperial Strength" (1905), *Our Own Islands: An Elementary Study in Geography* (1906), "On Thinking Imperially" (1907), "The Geographical Environment of Great Britain" (1908), *The Rhine: Its Valley and History* (1908), "Geographical Conditions Affecting the British Empire" (1909), "The Geographical Conditions of the Defence of the United Kingdom" (1909), "The New Map" (1915), "Some Geographical Aspects of

International Reconstruction" (1917), "This Unprecedented War" (1917), and "The New Map of Europe" (1918).

Shortly after the end of the First World War, Mackinder wrote *Democratic Ideals and Reality*, arguably the most important work on international politics ever written by a geographer. Here, Mackinder greatly expanded on his 1904 "pivot" paper, drawing on recent lessons learned from the Great War. In the book's preface, referring to the continuing relevance of the ideas expressed in the "pivot" paper, Mackinder opined that "the war has established, and not shaken, my former points of view." In the two hundred or so pages that followed, Mackinder presented a masterful synthesis of historical and geographical analyses that has withstood the test of time.

Early in the book, Mackinder emphasized the paramount importance of geography to the study of history and global politics. "The great wars of history," he wrote, "are the outcome, direct or indirect, of the unequal growth of nations, and that unequal growth... in large measure ... is the result of the uneven distribution of fertility and strategical opportunity upon the face of the globe."[25] The "facts of geography" indicated to Mackinder that "the grouping of lands and seas, and of fertility and natural pathways, is such as to lend itself to the growth of empires, and in the end of a single world empire."[26] In order to prevent future world conflicts, he advised, "we must recognize these geographical realities and take steps to counter their influence."[27] He proposed to reveal those "geographical realities" by measuring "the relative significance of the great features of our globe as tested by the events of history."[28]

Mackinder pointed out that although the "physical facts of geography have remained substantially the same during... recorded human history," it was only at the beginning of the twentieth century that the globe became, in political terms, a "closed system."[29] "Every shock, every disaster or superfluity," he wrote, "is now felt even to the antipodes.... Every deed of humanity will henceforth be echoed and re-echoed in like manner round the world."[30]

In geographical terms, Mackinder's world as sketched in *Democratic Ideals and Reality* consisted of the following: (1) one ocean covering nine-twelfths of the globe; (2) one great continent encompassing Europe, Asia, and Africa; and (3) several smaller islands including Britain, Japan, North America, South America, and Australia. The one great continent, which Mackinder called "the World-

Island," he further subdivided into six regions: the European coastland (Western and Central Europe), the Monsoon or Asian coastland (India, China, Southeast Asia, Korea, and eastern Siberia), Arabia (the Arabian peninsula), the Sahara (North Africa), the Southern Heartland (Africa south of the Sahara), and, most important, the Heartland (the northern-central core of Eurasia which he had called the "pivot region" in his 1904 paper).

Mackinder showed the significance of the position of the Eurasian-African "World-Island" on the globe by geo historical analogy. The "World-Island" was to North America, he explained, what Greece under the Dorians had been to Crete, and what the Roman Empire had been to Britain, that is, an unchallenged peninsular land power versus an insular sea power. In both of those instances of history, strongly based unchallenged land power defeated the less strongly based sea power. But it was not simply a case of land power being superior to sea power. The victorious land power had to be unchallenged by land, and had to possess sufficient resources to enable it to construct a fleet powerful enough to defeat the insular sea power. Absent those two conditions, a strongly based insular power would prevail, as evidenced by the British defeat of Napoleon's France, the latter of which, while possessing tremendous resources, faced a significant land power challenge to the east (Russia) which prevented it from harnessing those resources to overwhelm British sea power.

Indeed, in Mackinder's view, the optimum geographical position combined insularity with greater resources, and that was precisely the position of the "World-Island." Strategists, he explained, "must no longer think of Europe apart from Asia and Africa. The Old World has become insular, or in other words a unit, incomparably the largest geographical unit on our globe."[31] In the First World War, had Germany conquered Russia and France, "she would have established her sea-power on a wider base than any in history, and in fact on the widest possible base."[32] Although Germany lost the war, Mackinder cautioned, "must we not still reckon with the possibility that a large part of the Great Continent might some day be united under a single sway, and that an invincible sea-power might be based upon it?" "[T]hat," Mackinder wrote, " is the great ultimate threat to the world's liberty."[33]

The most strategically significant geographic feature of the "World-Island" was the Heartland, which Mackinder described as "a great continuous patch in the north and center of the continent... from the icy, flat shore of Siberia to the torrid, steep coasts of Baluchistan and Persia."[34] This region's great rivers (Lena, Yenisei, Obi, Volga, and Ural) emptied either into the frozen Arctic Ocean or inland seas (the Caspian and Aral), thereby rendering the Heartland "inaccessible to navigation from the ocean." The Heartland also included a great "lowland" plain that formed "a broad gateway from Siberia into Europe," which is suitable to highly mobile land power.[35]

As in his 1904 "pivot" paper, Mackinder in *Democratic Ideals and Reality*, used history to illustrate the strategic significance of geography. He noted that beginning with the Huns in the fifth century, successive waves of mobile hordes emerged from the Heartland to conquer or threaten the coastlands of Europe and Asia. Those hordes, however, lacked sufficient manpower and organization to conquer the whole World-Island, or a large part of it (although the Mongols came close to doing so). Two modern developments—increased population and advanced means of overland transportation (railroads, motorcars)—threatened to upset the balance between land power and sea power, and constituted, in Mackinder's words, "a revolution in the relations of man to the larger geographical realities of the world."[36]

Mackinder described how during the nineteenth century following the defeat of Napoleon and until the rise of the German empire, British sea power sought to contain Russian land power, a geopolitical struggle that has since been called the "great game." Germany's rise to world power after 1871 shifted the geopolitical focus of British statesmen and set the stage for the First World War. For Mackinder, the most important aspect of that war, for the purposes of strategy, was Germany's near successful conquest of Eastern Europe and the Heartland. Had Germany discarded the Schlieffen Plan, remained nominally at peace with France and Britain, and directed all her efforts and resources eastward, the world would be "overshadowed by a German East Europe in command of the Heartland." "The British and American insular peoples," warned Mackinder, "would not have realized the strategical danger until too late."[37]

Mackinder perceived a consistent geographical basis for British policy during the "great game" and the First World War. "We were opposed to the... Russian Czardom," explained Mackinder, "because Russia was the dominating, threatening force both in East Europe and the Heartland for a half century." "We were opposed to the...

German Kaiserdom, because Germany took the lead from the Czardom, and would have crushed the revolting Slavs, and dominated East Europe and the Heartland."[38] This strategic insight formed the basis of Mackinder's memorable advice to the Western statesmen at Versailles: "Who rules East Europe commands the Heartland: Who rules the Heartland commands the World-Island: Who rules the World-Island commands the World."[39]

The postwar settlement and reconstruction was the focus of the final part of *Democratic Ideals and Reality*. Mackinder worried that failure by the statesmen at Versailles to construct an effective security system for Eastern Europe would mean that after the terrible sufferings of the First World War, the Western democracies "shall merely have gained a respite, and our descendants will find themselves under the necessity of marshaling their power afresh for the siege of the Heartland."[40] To those who argued that Germany's defeat would alter the German desire for conquest and power, Mackinder sagely replied, "He would be a sanguine man ... who would trust the future peace of the world to a change in the mentality of any nation."[41] To those who argued that peace would be secured by the new League of Nations and its professed ideals, Mackinder prophetically remonstrated, "No mere scraps of paper, even though they be the written constitution of a League of Nations, are, under the conditions of to-day, a sufficient guarantee that the Heartland will not again become the center of a world war."[42]

Mackinder's proposed solution to the problem of Eastern Europe, which he derived from "a consideration of the realities presented by the geography of our globe,"[43] was the formation of a "tier of independent states between Germany and Russia," which would form "a broad wedge of independence, extending from the Adriatic and Black Seas to the Baltic."[44] This "territorial buffer between Germany and Russia," wrote Mackinder, must have access to the ocean, and must be supported by the "outer nations" (i.e., Britain and the United States).[45] Otherwise, the East European power vacuum would again serve as the spark to ignite yet another struggle for Eurasian hegemony.

During the 1920s and 1930s, unfortunately, Mackinder's ideas had little influence in Britain or the United States. That was not the case, however, in Germany where Mackinder's global view attracted the attention and praise of Karl Haushofer and his associates at Munich's Institute of Geopolitics. The German geopoliticians, influenced by the writings of Oswald Spengler, Friedrich Ratzel, and Rudolf Kjellen, adapted Mackinder's theories and concepts to promote German expansion. Haushofer in the 1920s and 1930s was close to Rudolf Hess, a close adviser to Hitler. But it is unclear to what extent the German geopoliticians influenced the *Fuhrer's* global strategy. Haushofer considered Mackinder the author of "the greatest of all geographical world views." "Never," exclaimed Haushofer referring to "The Geographical Pivot of History," "have I seen anything greater than these few pages of a geopolitical masterwork."[46] The German geopoliticians divided the world into "Pan Regions" each of which was dominated by a great power. Haushofer advocated the formation of a "Eurasiatic great continental bloc"; in essence, an alliance between Germany, Japan, and Russia that would eventually overwhelm the British Empire.[47]

During the interwar period, Mackinder was knighted (1920), lost his seat in Parliament (1922), chaired the Imperial Shipping Committee (1920-1939), sat on the Imperial Economic Committee (1925-1931), was made a Privy Councilor (1926), and continued to write and lecture on geography and related topics. His interwar writings included, "Geography as a Pivotal Subject in Education"(1921), "The Sub-Continent of India"(1922), *The Nations of the Modern World: An Elementary Study in Geography and History, After 1914* (1924), and "The Human Habitat"(1931).[48]

The Nazi-Soviet Pact of August 1939, the beginning of the Second World War and Germany's subsequent invasion of the Soviet Union drew attention in the United States to Mackinder's works. In 1941 and 1942, *Newsweek, Reader's Digest,* and *Life* published articles which prominently mentioned Mackinder and his writings. *Democratic Ideals and Reality* was reprinted in 1942. That same year, Hamilton Fish Armstrong, the editor of *Foreign Affairs,* asked Mackinder to write an article to update his Heartland theory. That article, entitled "The Round World and the Winning of the Peace," appeared in July 1943, and was Mackinder's last significant statement of his global views.

"[M]y concept of the Heartland," wrote Mackinder, "is more valid and useful today than it was either twenty or forty years ago."[49] He described the Heartland in geographical terms as "the northern part and the interior of Euro-Asia," extending "from the Arctic coast down to the central deserts," flowing westward to "the broad isthmus between the Baltic and Black Seas."[50] The Heartland concept, he explained, is based on "three separate aspects of physical geography." First, "the widest lowland plain on the face of the globe." Second, "great navigable rivers [that] flow across that plain [but have] no access to the ocean." And third, "a grassland zone which ... presented ideal conditions for the development of high mobility" by land transportation.[51] The Heartland, in essence, wrote Mackinder, was equivalent to the territory of the Soviet Union, minus the land east of the Yenisei River.

If the Soviet Union defeated Germany in the war, opined Mackinder, "she must rank as the greatest land Power on the globe."[52] 'The Heartland is the greatest natural fortress on earth,' he explained, and "[f]or the first time in history it is manned by a garrison sufficient both in number and quality."[53]

A second geographical feature which Mackinder estimated to be "of almost equal significance" to the Heartland was the "Midland Ocean," consisting of the eastern half of Canada and the United States, the North Atlantic basin and its "four subsidiaries (Mediterranean, Baltic, Arctic, and Caribbean Seas)," Britain and France (a remarkable description of the NATO alliance that was formed six years *after* Mackinder wrote his article).[54]

Completing his updated global sketch, Mackinder identified three additional geographic features. The first was "a girdle of deserts and wildernesses" extending from the Sahara Desert eastward to Arabia, Tibet, and Mongolia to eastern Siberia, Alaska, part of Canada and the western United States.[55] The second consisted of South America, the South Atlantic Ocean and Africa. And the third encompassed the "Monsoon lands" of China and India.[56] He expressed the hope that those lands would prosper and, thereby, balance the other regions of the globe. "A balanced globe of human beings," he wrote, "[a]nd happy, because balanced and thus free."[57]

Mackinder expressed the hope that Heartland Russia would cooperate with the Midland Ocean powers in the postwar world and, thereby, prevent future German aggression. But his theories and concepts proved readily adaptable to the emerging Cold War struggle between the United States and the Soviet Union. American strategists during and after the Second World War borrowed aspects of Mackinder's worldview in formulating and implementing the policy of "containment" of Soviet Russia.[58] Anthony J. Pierce, in his introduction to the 1962 edition of *Democratic Ideals and Reality*, could confidently assert that "[i]n America and in England, since 1942, most studies of global strategy or political geography have been based, in whole or in part, upon [Mackinder's] theories."[59] Mackinder, of course, had his share of critics,[60] but as Colin Gray has pointed out, "Mackinder's interpretations of historically shifting power relationships in their geographical setting have stood the test of time much better than have the slings and arrows of his legion of critics."[61]

More recent and current political observers and strategists attest to the continuing influence of Mackinder's ideas. In 1974, R. E. Walters wrote that "the Heartland theory stands as the first premise in Western military thought."[62] In 1975, Saul B. Cohen noted that "most Western strategists continue to view the world as initially described by Mackinder."[63] Zbigniew Brzezinski's *Game Plan* (1986) and *The Grand Chessboard* (1997) present global views almost wholly based on Mackinder's concepts. In 1980, Robert Nisbet claimed that "[e]very geopolitical apprehension that Sir Halford Mackinder expressed some six decades ago in his *Democratic Ideals and Reality* has been fulfilled."[64] The influential journals, *Strategic Review* and the *National Interest*, published several articles in the 1980s and 1990s wherein the authors applied Mackinder's theories and concepts to contemporary global issues.[65] In 1988, the respected strategist Colin Gray asserted that "[t]he geopolitical ideas of the British geographer Sir Halford Mackinder ... provide an intellectual architecture, far superior to rival conceptions, for understanding the principal international security issues."[66] In 1994, the former State Department Geographer, George J. Demko, wrote that "the geographic ideas of ... Mackinder, still provide important insights into international political processes."[67] Henry Kissinger in his book, *Diplomacy* (1994), concludes with a warning that "Russia, regardless of who governs it, sits astride territory Halford Mackinder called the geopolitical heartland...."[68] Paul Kennedy, Robert Chase, and Emily Hill invoked Mackinder's theories in a 1996 *Foreign Affairs* article on post-Cold War "pivot states."[69] Finally, in 1996 the National Defense University issued a reprint of *Democratic Ideals and Reality*.

Twentieth-century global politics were shaped, in part, by Mackinder's geopolitical vision. Following his concepts, the continuing struggle for Eurasian mastery was the geopolitical essence of the First World War, the Second World War, and the Cold War. First Great Britain, then the United States, organized great coalitions to oppose successive bids for Eurasian hegemony launched by Wilhelmine Germany, Nazi Germany, and the Soviet Union. The Great Power struggles of the twenty-first century will likely repeat this pattern.

The People's Republic of China, situated at the gates of Mackinder's "pivot region" or Heartland, and with access to the sea, possesses sufficient human and natural resources to make a bid for Eurasian mastery sometime in this new century. Russia, though currently undergoing a new time of troubles, still occupies the Heartland and possesses vast human and natural resources, as well as thousands of nuclear weapons. The nations of Western, Central and Eastern Europe are moving toward economic unity and, perhaps, political unity, with Germany playing a leading role. Whatever specific power constellation emerges, however, U.S. foreign policy will continue to be shaped by Mackinder's geopolitical vision of a Eurasian-based world hegemon.

In 1944, the American Geographical Society awarded Mackinder the Charles P. Daley Medal, which was presented to him at the American Embassy on March 31, 1944. Ambassador John Winant remarked that Mackinder was "the first who fully enlisted geography as an aid to statecraft and strategy."[70] A year later, the Royal Geographical Society awarded Mackinder the Patron's Medal, and its president noted that "[a]s a political geographer his reputation is ... world wide."[71] Mackinder died on March 6, 1947 at the age of eighty-six. More than fifty years later, as we enter a new century, statesmen and strategists still operate in Mackinder's world.

Notes

1.   W. H. Parker, *Mackinder: Geography as an Aid to Statecraft* (Oxford: Clarendon Press), pp. 1-2.
2.   Brian W. Blouet, *Halford Mackinder: A Biography* (College Station,Texas: Texas A&M University Press, 1987), p. 33.
3.   Parker, *Mackinder*, p.8.
4.   Halford J. Mackinder, "On the Scope and Methods of Geography," in *Democratic Ideals and Reality* (New York: W. W. Norton & Company,1962), pp. 213, 214, 217.
5.   Mackinder, "On the Scope and Methods of Geography," pp. 211, 218, 236, 237.
6.   The details of Mackinder's education and teaching positions are found in Parker, *Mackinder: Geography as an Aid to Statecraft*, pp. 28-102, and Blouet, *Mackinder: A Biography*.
7.   Halford Mackinder, *Britain and the British Seas* (Westport, CT: Greenwood Press Publishers, 1969, originally published in 1902 by D. Appleton and Company), p.vii.
8.   Ibid., p. 12.

9. Ibid., p. 12.
10. Ibid., pp. 350-351.
11. Ibid., p. 358.
12. Halford J. Mackinder, "The Geographical Pivot of History," in *Democratic Ideals and Reality*, p. 241.
13. Ibid., pp. 241-242.
14. Ibid., p. 242.
15. Ibid., p. 242.
16. Ibid., p. 255.
17. Ibid., p. 257-258.
18. Ibid., p. 258.
19. Ibid., p. 262.
20. Ibid., p. 264.
21. Ibid., p. 263.
22. Parker, *Mackinder: Geography as an Aid to Statecraft*, p. 149.
23. Ibid., p. 158.
24. Ibid., p. 170.
25. *Democratic Ideals and Reality*, pp. 1-2.
26. Ibid., p. 2.
27. Ibid., p. 2.
28. Ibid., p. 4.
29. Ibid., pp. 28-29.
30. Ibid., pp. 29-30.
31. Ibid., pp. 65-66.
32. Ibid., p. 62.
33. Ibid., p. 70.
34. Ibid., p. 73.
35. Ibid., p. 74.
36. Ibid., pp. 73-74.
37. Ibid., p. 150.
38. Ibid., p. 139.
39. Ibid., p. 150.
40. Ibid., p. 154.
41. Ibid., p. 155.
42. Ibid., p. 114.
43. Ibid., p. 182.
44. Ibid., pp. 158, 165.
45. Ibid., p. 160.
46. Hans W. Weigert, *Generals and Geographers: The Twilight of Geopolitics* (New York: Oxford University Press, 1942), p. 116.
47. Ibid., p. 186.
48. See Blouet, op. cit. At pp. 207-215.
49. "The Round World and the Winning of the Peace," in *Democratic Ideals and Reality*, op. cit., p. 276.
50. Ibid., p. 268.
51. Ibid., pp. 268-269.
52. Ibid., pp. 272-273.
53. Ibid., p. 273.
54. Ibid., pp. 275, 277.
55. Ibid., pp. 274-275.
56. Ibid., pp. 277-278.
57. Ibid., p. 278.

58.   Among those strategists were Nicholas Spykman, James Burnham, George Kennan, Edward Mead Earle, General Omar Bradley, and William C. Bullitt.

59.   *Democratic Ideals and Reality*, p. xxi.

60.   For an excellent summary of criticisms of Mackinder, see Parker, *Geography as an Aid to Statecraft*, pp. 211-247.

61.   Colin S. Gray, *The Geopolitics of Super Power* (Lexington: The University Press of Kentucky, 1988), p. 4.

62.   Quoted in Parker, *Geography as an Aid to Statecraft*, p. 192.

63.   Saul B. Cohen, *Geography and Politics in a World Divided* (New York: Oxford University Press, 1975), p. 44.

64.   Robert Nisbet, *History of the Idea of Progress* (New York: Basic Books, Inc., 1980), p. 331.

65.   See, for example, Eugene V. Rostow, "Of Summitry and Grand Strategy," *Strategic Review* (Fall 1986), pp. 9-20; Francis P. Sempa, "Geopolitics and American Strategy: A Reassessment," *Strategic Review* (Spring 1987), pp. 27-38; William C. Bodie, "The American Strategy Schism," *Strategic Review* (Spring 1988), pp. 9-15; Mackubin Thomas Owens, "Force Planning in an Era of Uncertainty," *Strategic Review* (Spring 1990), pp. 9-22; Henry C. Bartlett and G. Paul Holman, "Force Planning for the Post-Cold War World: What Can We Learn From Geopolitics," *Strategic Review* (Winter 1991), pp. 26-36; Francis P. Sempa, "The Geopolitics of the Post-Cold War World," *Strategic Review* (Winter 1992), pp. 9-18; Mackubin Thomas Owens, "Toward a Maritime Grand Strategy: Paradigm for a New Security Environment," *Strategic Review* (Spring 1993), pp. 7-19; Francis P. Sempa, "Preventive Containment," *Strategic Review* (Summer 1994), pp. 83-85; Colin S. Gray, "NATO: In Trouble at the Crossroads Again," *Strategic Review* (Summer 1995), pp. 7-15; Francis P. Sempa, "Central and Eastern Europe," *Strategic Review* (Fall 1996), pp. 71-72; Francis P. Sempa, review of *The Grand Chessboard* in *Strategic Review* (Spring 1998), pp. 71-74; Colin S. Gray, "Keeping the Soviets Landlocked: Geostrategy for a Maritime America," *National Interest* (Summer 1986), pp. 24-36; Francis P. Sempa, "The Geopolitics Man," *National Interest* (Fall 1992), pp. 96-102.

66.   Colin S. Gray, *The Geopolitics of Super Power*, p.4.

67.   George J. Demko and William B. Wood, ed. *Reordering the World: Geopolitical Perspectives on the 21st Century* (Boulder, CO: Westview Press, 1994), p. 4.

68.   Henry Kissinger, *Diplomacy* (New York: Simon and Schuster, 1994), p. 814.

69.   "Pivotal States and U.S. Strategy," January/February 1996 *Foreign Affairs*.

70.   Parker, *Mackinder: Geography as an Aid to Statecraft*, p. 54.

71.   Ibid., p. 55.

3

The Geopolitics Man

For over forty years, the United States adhered to a foreign policy dominated by one overriding goal: the containment of Soviet power within the geographical borders established at the end of the Second World War. Although American statesmen frequently expressed the underpinnings of the containment policy in ideological terms—democracy and freedom vs. communism—the policy's practical moorings were geopolitical. Thus, the U.S. fought Communist China (during the Korean War) when the latter was allied to Moscow, but cooperated with the same totalitarian regime after the Sino-Soviet split. Similarly, the U.S. cozied up to Yugoslavian and Romanian communists when their regimes distanced themselves from Moscow's foreign policies.

Cooperation with anti-Soviet communist regimes was only one aspect of America's Cold War policy that betrayed its ideological façade. The U.S. also found it expedient to form alliances or cooperate with authoritarian dictatorships that were situated in key strategic areas around the globe. Thus, the United States courted South Korean, South Vietnamese, and Nicaraguan authoritarian rulers who opposed Soviet proxies, and allied itself to princes, sheiks, and shahs who opposed Soviet encroachments in the Middle East.

Contrary to popular opinion, the Cold War was fought not over democratic ideals, but because of geopolitical realities. The United States opposed the Soviet Union because it threatened U.S. strategic interests, not because the Soviet regime denied freedom and democracy to its citizens. The balance of power, rather than ideological sentiment, guided U.S. foreign policy during the Cold War.

It is fashionable to trace the intellectual roots of America's containment policy to George F. Kennan's "long telegram" from Moscow in 1946 and his "X" article in *Foreign Affairs* the following year. Kennan's perceptive analyses and prudent policy proposals, however, were not written in an intellectual vacuum. Forty-two years before Kennan wrote his "long telegram," a British geographer, Halford Mackinder, produced a brilliant geopolitical analysis that established the theoretical basis for America's containment policy.

In "The Geographical Pivot of History," presented to London's Royal Geographical Society in 1904, Mackinder identified the northern-central core of the Eurasian landmass as the "pivot region" from which a sufficiently armed and organized great power could threaten world domination. Because of its geographical location, the "pivot region" enabled its occupant to expand westward into the European peninsula, eastward into the far reaches of Siberia and East Asia, and southward into the Middle East and south-central Asia. Mackinder referred to the contiguous lands abutting the "pivot region" as the "inner or marginal crescent." Together, the "pivot region" and the lands of the "inner or marginal crescent" contained the bulk of the earth's population and resources and formed the great continent of "Euro-Asia."[1]

Mackinder's study of the geography of the "pivot region" revealed three striking characteristics. First, the "pivot region" consisted largely of a vast, unbroken lowland plain that is suitable to highly mobile land power. Second, the pivot state could expand into the marginal lands of Eurasia without crossing any significant body of water, that is, without using sea power. Third, the "pivot region" was itself impenetrable to sea power since its major rivers emptied into inland seas or the frozen Arctic Ocean. Geography had thus formed a natural citadel for mobile land power and placed it in the strategically most advantageous region of the earth's dominant landmass.

Mackinder completed his global sketch by placing Great Britain, North and South America, Southern Africa, and Australia in the "outer or insular crescent." He then warned,

> The oversetting of the balance of power in favor of the pivot state, resulting in its expansion over the marginal lands of Euro-Asia, would permit the use of vast continental resources for fleet-building, and the empire of the world would then be in sight. [2]

The main contenders for world empire, according to Mackinder, were Russia, Germany (or an alliance of the two) and, possibly, a Sino-Japanese alliance.

Mackinder's conception resulted from a masterful fusion of historical, geographical, technological, demographic, and economic factors. History revealed that the steppes of the pivot region had hosted a series of nomadic peoples (Huns, Avars, Magyars, Cumans, Bulgarians, Khazars, Patzthaks, Kalmuks, and Mongols) who "emerged from...the broad interval between the Ural mountains and the Caspian sea, rode through the open spaces of southern Russia, and struck home into...the very heart of the European peninsula."[3] He attached special significance to the Mongol conquests of the thirteenth and fourteenth centuries, when "all the settled margins of the Old World sooner or later felt the expansive force of mobile power originating in the steppe. Russia, Persia, India, and China were either made tributary, or received Mongol dynasties."[4] Mackinder saw Russia as the successor to the Mongol empire, capable of exerting pressure from the pivot region into the heavily populated and resource-rich regions of the "inner or marginal crescent" of Eurasia.

Mackinder was not the first observer to note Russia's potential as the world's dominant land power. The noted American naval historian and strategist, Alfred Thayer Mahan, had advanced a similar, if less grandiose, thesis four years earlier in his book, *The Problem of Asia.*[5] Where Mackinder broke new ground, however, was in his breathtaking geohistorical analysis, as well as his keen appreciation of the impending technological developments that would give land powers distinct strategic advantages over sea powers. Railways and motor cars were destined to increase land power's speed and mobility exponentially. The wonders of the Industrial Revolution would speed economic development, enhance military power and flexibility, and expand the potential reach of political control. The pivot state's geographical advantages would be enhanced by technological change. The era of dominant sea powers was coming to a close.[6]

Mackinder's prediction of the ascendency of land power was not particularly welcomed in his own country, whose navy had ruled the waves for several centuries. Englishmen preferred the writings of the American Mahan, which celebrated British sea power and its accomplishments in crafting and maintaining a worldwide empire over which the sun never set. That empire would soon expend the blood of its youth in a successful coalition effort to stave off an attempt at European hegemony by Imperial Germany.

World War I resulted in the collapse of four imperial regimes, the physical break-up of three empires, the creation of a world forum for international disputes, the rise of extremist ideological movements in Europe and Asia, and America's entry into the ranks of the great powers. In the wake of those dramatic political changes and the defeat of German land power, however, Mackinder sensed a reaffirmation of the geopolitical concepts he formulated in 1904. In the preface to his landmark postwar book, *Democratic Ideals and Reality*, Mackinder wrote that the war had "established, and not shaken, my former points of view."[7]

Mackinder began this seminal work with the observation that "the great wars of history...are the outcome, direct or indirect, of the unequal growth of nations, and that unequal growth...is the result of the uneven distribution of fertility and strategical opportunity upon the face of the globe." [8] The facts of geography revealed to Mackinder that "the grouping of lands and seas, and of fertility and natural pathways, is such as to lend itself to the growth of empires, and in the end of a single world empire."[9] Mackinder's avowed purposes in writing this book were to help the Western democracies (especially Great Britain) "recognize these geographical realities," persuade Western statesmen to "take steps to counter their influence," and enable democratic leaders to determine "how we may best adjust our ideals of freedom to these lasting realities of our earthly home."[10]

In the first part of *Democratic Ideals and Reality*, Mackinder reviewed the geographical setting of the historical struggles for power and dominion between insular sea powers and peninsular land powers: Crete vs. Greece; Celtic Britain vs. Rome; Great Britain vs. European continental powers. His study of those conflicts revealed three common geopolitical insights:(1) sea power depends on secure and resourceful land bases; (2) a peninsular land power, freed from challenges by other land powers and commanding greater resources, can defeat insular sea powers; and (3) the optimum strategic position is one combining insularity and greater resources.

Mackinder took these geopolitical insights and applied them to a strategic map of the world. He believed that the entire globe was the proper field of geopolitical study and analysis because "we are now for the first time presented with a closed political system." "Every shock, every disaster or superfluity," he wrote, "is now felt even to the antipodes.... Every deed of humanity will henceforth be echoed and re-echoed in like manner round the world."[11]

The world, according to Mackinder, consisted of three essential elements: one ocean covering nine-twelfths of the earth; one great continent composed of Europe, Asia and Africa covering two-twelfths of the earth; and several smaller islands making up the remaining one-twelfth of the earth. He called the one great continent the "world promontory" or "World-Island." The Eurasian-African World-Island contained most of the world's people and resources, and it had the additional characteristic of potential insularity. It thus possessed the two features that defined Mackinder's optimum strategic position. A great land power in command of the vast resources of the World-Island, and freed from serious challenges by other land powers, could also become the world's preeminent sea power. In Mackinder's own ominous words,

> [M]ust we not still reckon with the possibility that a large part of the Great Continent might some day be united under a single sway, and that an invincible sea-power might be based upon it? .... Ought we not to recognize that that is the great ultimate threat to the world's liberty so far as strategy is concerned, and to provide against it in our new political systems?[12]

After presenting geopolitical factors that pointed to the potential for a world imperium, Mackinder addressed the question of the potential seat of world empire. Here, he expanded directly on his 1904 address to the Royal Geographical Society. He used different terms—the "pivot region" was renamed the "Heartland," the lands of the "inner or marginal crescent" became the Eurasian "coastlands"—but the grand conception remained, in its essentials, the same as in 1904. The boundaries of the "pivot region" or "Heartland" were altered slightly. Again, but with greater detail, Mackinder recounted the succession of mobile, horse-riding peoples (Huns, Avars, Magyars, Tartars, Turks, and Cossacks) who emerged from the inner-recesses of Asia to conquer lands to the west and south. Again, he described the geographical details that made the Heartland impenetrable to sea power. Mackinder acknowledged the failure of previous Heartland-based empires to achieve world dominion (though the Mongols came uncomfortably close to conquering the known world), but he attributed this to an insufficient base of manpower and a lack of relative mobility vis-à-vis sea powers. In the twentieth century, according to Mackinder, those two obstacles to a Heartland-based world empire no longer existed, and this fact "constitut[ed] a revolution in the relations of men to the larger geographical realities of the world."[13]

Having established the geohistorical framework, Mackinder analyzed the "great game" of the nineteenth century that pitted British sea power against Russian land power based in the Heartland. The following geopolitical description of that competition in *Democratic Ideals and Reality* is vintage Mackinder:

> Russia, in command of nearly the whole of the Heartland, was knocking at the landward gates of the Indies. Britain, on the other hand, was knocking at the sea gates of China, and advancing inland from the sea gates of India to meet the menace from the northwest. Russian rule in the Heartland was based on her man-power in East Europe, and was carried to the gates of the Indies by the mobility of the Cossack cavalry. British power along the sea frontage of the Indies was based on the man-power of the distant islands in Western Europe, and was made available in the East by the mobility of British ships.[14]

Russia also exerted pressure on the Balkans, seeking to 'extend her land power to the Dardenelles,'' and this, too, brought forth opposition from Britain and France.[15] Although Mackinder never used the term, British policy toward Russia throughout much of the nineteenth century could accurately be described as "containment." Britain utilized her alliances and, above all, her sea power to oppose Russian encroachments in the Indies and the Balkans.

The unification of Germany in 1871 under the skillful leadership of Otto von Bismarck created a new contender for continental hegemony. The new German nation possessed a large and growing population, industrial might, a Prussian ruling caste that had great knowledge of, and interest in, geography, a tendency toward militarism, and, perhaps most important, a talent for organizing manpower. The new Germany was, in Mackinder's phrase, a "Going Concern."

Imperial Germany made a bid for continental hegemony between 1914 and 1918, and almost succeeded. Her victory over Russia in the east, however, was cut short and rendered ineffectual by her defeat in the west; a defeat, it must be emphasized, that was made possible only by American intervention. Germany's fundamental strategic error, in Mackinder's view, was her attempt to conquer France and Britain before she had *effectively* commanded and organized the resources of Eastern Europe and the Heartland:

> Had Germany elected to stand on the defensive on her short frontier towards France, and had she thrown her main strength against Russia, it is not improbable that the world would be nominally at peace today, but overshadowed by a German East Europe in command of all of the Heartland. The British and American insular peoples would not have realized the strategical danger until too late.[16]

Had Germany won World War I, Mackinder warned, "she would have established her sea power on a wider base than any in history, and in fact on the widest possible base."[17] In other words, a Ger-

many victorious on the continent could have utilized its newly conquered resources to build the world's most powerful navy and overwhelm the remaining insular powers (Britain and the United States).

The facts of geography, the historic rivalry of empires, and the
geopolitical lessons of the First World War convinced Mackinder of
the strategic necessity to prevent the consolidation of Eastern Europe and the Heartland by a single power or alliance of powers.
Failure to do so could produce a great power that was supreme both
on land and at sea. This reasoning and apprehension formed the
basis of Mackinder's famous warning to the peacemakers at Versailles:

Who rules East Europe commands the Heartland:

Who rules the Heartland commands the World-Island:

Who rules the World-Island commands the World.[18]

Mackinder proposed erecting "a tier of independent states between
Germany and Russia" to act as a buffer separating the two great
powers.[19] That, of course, is exactly what the peacemakers did after
the war, but it did not prevent a second global conflict. Mackinder's
later critics were quick to point out this "flaw" in his analysis. What
the critics failed to note, however, was that Mackinder never believed that a "tier of independent states" in Eastern Europe, alone,
could prevent another bid for continental supremacy. He knew and
wrote that to be an effective geopolitical buffer, the East European
states would have to cooperate with each other in the face of common threats from east or west, and would require the support of
Britain, France, *and the United States*—support that never material-
ized in the 1930s. We can never know for certain whether early and
effective Western support for Czechoslovakia, Austria, and Poland
would have deterred Hitler and prevented the outbreak of World
War II. We do know that Winston Churchill thought so.[20]

Mackinder wrote from the perspectives of a scholar and a statesman. Born in Lancashire, England in 1861, Mackinder studied geography, history, and economics, and served as a member of Parliament from 1910-1922. He served as Britain's High Commissioner
for South Russia in 1919-1920 during Russia's civil war, and later
chaired the Imperial Shipping Committee and the Imperial Economic
Committee. He was made a privy councilor in 1925.[21]

Ironically, in spite of his distinguished scholarly and political career in Britain, Mackinder's geopolitical theories found a more re-

ceptive audience in foreign lands, particularly Germany. Germany, of course, was the birthplace of scientific political geography. Immanuel Kant lectured extensively on "physical geography" at the University of Konigsberg as early as 1756. Shortly thereafter, Johann Cristoph Gatterer theorized that the world could be divided into "natural" regions and lands. The early nineteenth century brought forth the systemic geographical studies of the "founders of modern geography," Alexander von Humboldt and Carl Ritter. Friedrich Ratzel, the "founder of modern political geography," focused his early twentieth-century writings on the concepts of space (*Raum*) and location (*Lage*) and their effects on the political lives of states.[22] Ratzel viewed the state as an "organism," and advised statesmen that "a healthy political instinct... means a correct evaluation of the geographic bases of political power."[23]

Germany, then, provided a fertile intellectual climate for Mackinder's geopolitical ideas, particularly after its humiliating defeat in the First World War. Dr. Karl Haushofer, a retired brigadier general and professor of geography at the University of Munich, founded the school of *Geopolitik* which studied the theories of Mackinder, Ratzel, and the Swedish political scientist Rudolf Kjellen. The German geopoliticians preached expansionism and world dominion, coining the term *Lebensraum* (living space) which became the rhetorical justification for Hitler's plan of conquest. In fact, Hitler was introduced to Haushofer in the 1920s by their mutual friend, Rudolf Hess. Portions of Hitler's *Mein Kampf* clearly evidence the influence of Haushofer and his followers.

The German geopoliticians preached autarky or national self-sufficiency, and they divided the world into "pan-regions" (Pan-America, Pan-Eurafrica, Pan-Russia and the Greater East Asia Co-prosperity Sphere). Haushofer considered Mackinder "the author of 'the greatest of all geographical world views.'" Haushofer advocated German mastery over Eurasia-Africa by conquest in the west and by agreement, if possible, with Russia in the east. He counseled against Germany's invasion of the Soviet Union in 1941, and ended up in Dachau in 1944. Haushofer's son was executed by the Nazis after being implicated in a plot to kill Hitler. Interestingly, Haushofer for a time sent geopolitical advice to Josef Stalin and to the Japanese militarists.[24]

Mackinder's warning in *Democratic Ideals and Reality* of another contest for Eurasian domination between Germany and Russia proved all too prophetic. But Hitler made the same mistakes the Kaiser did twenty-five years earlier: he waged war in the west before he had sufficiently conquered and organized the resources of Eastern Europe and the Heartland, and he pursued policies that brought the United States into the war.

During the war (1943), Mackinder was asked by the editors of *Foreign Affairs* to revisit his Heartland thesis. As he wrote, the tide of the war had turned in the Allies' favor. German land power was on the verge of defeat. To American and British observers it seemed that sea power had once again triumphed over land power, thus calling into question the validity of Mackinder's theory. Such a conclusion, however, ignored the crucial contribution of Soviet Russia to Germany's defeat. It was a combination of Western sea power and Russian land power that brought down the Third Reich.

Mackinder's article, entitled "The Round World and the Winning of the Peace," was forward looking.[25] He assumed that Germany's defeat was inevitable, and he expressed confidence in the soundness of his original conception. "[M]y concept of the Heartland," he wrote,"...is more valid and useful today than it was either twenty or forty years ago."[26] For practical purposes he described the boundaries of the Heartland as being roughly coterminous to the Soviet Union, except for a large stretch of territory surrounding the river Lena in eastern Siberia which Mackinder excluded from the Heartland. He concluded that a victorious Soviet Union would "emerge from this war... as the greatest land power on the globe." He described the Heartland as "the greatest natural fortress on earth," and he noted that "for the first time in history it is manned by a garrison sufficient both in number and quality."[27]

Balancing the dominant land power of the Heartland and the potential threat of a revived Germany was Mackinder's second great geopolitical concept: the "Midland Ocean," which consisted of peninsular Western Europe, Britain, the Atlantic Ocean and eastern Canada and the United States. He judged the Midland Ocean to be a geopolitical feature "of almost equal significance" to the Heartland.[28] Perceptive readers will undoubtedly notice the similarities between Mackinder's Midland Ocean and the North Atlantic Treaty Organization, which was formed in 1949 precisely for the purpose of counterbalancing Soviet Heartland power.

It would be difficult to overestimate the impact of *Democratic Ideals and Reality* on the thinking of Western strategists. It was reprinted in 1942 and 1962, and its concepts influenced the writings of James Burnham, Nicholas Spykman, Walter Lippmann, Raymond Aron, Robert Strausz-Hupé, Hans Weigert and other postwar strategists. In the introduction to the 1962 edition, Anthony J. Pierce described *Democratic Ideals and Reality* as "a masterly analysis of the permanent strategic factors which have governed all struggles for world empire," and he noted that "in America and in England, since 1942, most studies of global strategy or political geography have been based, in whole or in part, upon Mackinder's theories."[29]

To be sure, Mackinder's writings produced many critics who focused on minor or insignificant details of his analysis that proved erroneous, or who ignored the qualifications and modifications that he made to his theory over time. But, as Colin Gray has pointed out, "Mackinder's interpretations of historically shifting power relationships in their geographical setting have stood the test of time much better than the slings and arrows of his legion of critics."[30]

One of the more persistent criticisms of Mackinder's writings is that they were too narrowly focused. Geography, although important, said the critics, was just one of many factors that influence world politics. In the critics' view, Mackinder's misplaced emphasis on geography led him to neglect or ignore other, perhaps more important, factors such as technological change and the impact of social and political organization. In fact, shortly after Mackinder delivered his 1904 paper on "The Geographical Pivot of History," the distinguished British statesman, Leo Amery, suggested that a nation's industrial might could render less meaningful its geographical position and the sea-power/land-power dichotomy.[31]

Here again, however, the critics have unfairly simplified Mackinder's views. While it is surely true that geographical factors were accorded primary importance by Mackinder, nevertheless, as early as 1904 he indicated that the balance of power was "the product, on the one hand, of geographical conditions, both economic and strategic, and, on the other hand, of the relative number, virility, equipment, and organization of the competing peoples..." He added, however, that "the geographical quantities in the calculation are more measurable and more nearly constant than the human."[32]

Far from ignoring the impact of technological change on the global balance of power, Mackinder grasped, before most of his contemporaries, that technology would improve the political and economic cohesiveness of continental-size states, and would give certain strategic advantages to land power vis-à-vis sea power.[33] In Mackinder's concept, geographical position provides the *opportunity* for the Heartland-based power to expand, while social and political organization and technology provide the *ability* and wherewithal for that power to harness resources and expand. The Soviet Union failed to win the Cold War because its geographical advantage was more than offset by its crumbling political and social organization in the face of determined Western containment.

Time has not lessened the relevance of Mackinder's concepts to the study and practice of international relations. The ideas first formulated in 1904, later expanded in *Democratic Ideals and Reality*, and fine-tuned in Mackinder's *Foreign Affairs* article, still influence some of our nation's most respected strategists.[34] His concepts and theories, in Colin Gray's words, "provide an intellectual architecture, far superior to rival conceptions, for understanding the principal international security issues."[35]

In the post-Cold War world, the Russian Republic still holds sway over most of the Heartland and is rich in natural and human resources. Germany is again united, an economic powerhouse situated in the center of Europe. In the Far East, China stands at the gateway to the Heartland with vast human resources, economic potential and access to the ocean, while Japan hints at playing a global role equal to its burgeoning economic power. With Germany taking the lead role in financing Russian reconstruction, and Japan increasing its economic and political ties to China, there is much to recommend in Mackinder's 1904 suggestion that the Heartland could at some future time be commanded and organized by a German-Russian condominium or a Sino-Japanese alliance.[36] While it is true that Japan and half of Germany have been stable democracies for over forty years, and Russia is currently experimenting with some democratic processes, it would be shortsighted for the United States to base its long-term security on the current political systems of powerful countries that have access to the major power centers of Eurasia. That is what Mackinder meant when he wrote in 1919: "He would be a sanguine man. . .who would trust the future peace of the world to a change in the mentality of any nation."[37]

Notes

1.   Mackinder's 1904 article is included in the 1962 edition of *Democratic Ideals and Reality* (New York: W.W. Norton & Co., Inc., 1962), pp. 241-264.

2. Ibid., p. 262.
3. Ibid., pp. 249-250.
4. Ibid., p. 254.
5. *The Problem of Asia* (Boston: Little, Brown and Co., 1900).
6. Three years earlier, in *Britain and the British Seas*, Mackinder commented that, "Other empires have had their days, and so may that of Britain."
7. Mackinder, *Democratic Ideals and Reality*, p. xxv.
8. Ibid., pp. 1-2.
9. Ibid., p. 2.
10. Ibid., pp. 2, 4.
11. Ibid., pp. 29-30.
12. Ibid., p. 70.
13. Ibid., pp. 73-74.
14. Ibid., p. 134.
15. Ibid., p. 136.
16. Ibid., pp. 149-150.
17. Ibid., p. 62.
18. Ibid., p. 150.
19. Ibid., p. 158.
20. Churchill's views on this matter are discussed at length in the first volume of his history of the Second World War, *The Gathering Storm* (Boston: Houghton Mifflin Company, 1948).
21. Biographical data on Mackinder can be found in Anthony J. Pearce's introduction to the 1962 edition of *Democratic Ideals and Reality*, pp. ix-xxiv; and W.H. Parker, *Mackinder: Geography as an Aid to Statecraft* (Oxford: Clarendon Press, 1982). 22. For a discussion of the study and teaching of physical and political geography in the German states, and later in Germany, see Richard Hartshorne, *The Nature of Geography* (Westport, CT: Greenwood Press, 1977).
23. Quoted in Nicholas Spykman, *America's Strategy in World Politics* (New York: Harcourt, Brace, 1942), p. 165.
24. For a discussion of the German geopoliticians and their impact on Hitler, see Derwent Whittlesy, "Haushofer: The Geopoliticians," in Edward Meade Earle, ed., *Makers of Modern Strategy: Military Thought from Machiavelli to Hitler* (Princeton, NJ: Princeton University Press, 1971), pp. 388-411.
25. Mackinder's 1943 *Foreign Affairs* article is also included in the 1962 edition of *Democratic Ideals and Reality*, pp. 265-278.
26. Mackinder, *Democratic Ideals and Reality*, p. 276.
27. Ibid., pp. 272-273.
28. Ibid., p. 275.
29. Ibid., pp. ix-xxi.
30. Colin S. Gray, *The Geopolitics of Super Power* (Lexington: The University Press of Kentucky, 1988), p.4.
31. For a good discussion of the major criticisms of Mackinder's geopolitical writings, see W.H. Parker, *Mackinder: Geography as an Aid to Statecraft*, pp. 213-247.
32. Mackinder, *Democratic Ideals and Reality*, p. 263.
33. Airpower enthusiasts have long claimed that the invention of the airplane added a wholly independent and potentially decisive dimension to warfare. In his 1943 essay in *Foreign Affairs*, Mackinder expressed the view that airpower depended on the "efficiency of its ground organization," and added that "no adequate proof has yet been presented that air fighting will not follow the long history of all kinds of warfare by presenting alternations of offensive and defensive tactical superiority, meanwhile effecting few permanent changes in strategical conditions." Ibid., p. 274.

Events since then, especially the Vietnam War, weigh heavily on the side of Mackinder's view. Even during the recent Persian Gulf War where airpower inflicted such devastation on Iraqi forces, our command of the seas and of an adequate land base were essential to transporting aircraft and missiles to the region and launching them after they had arrived. Furthermore, the Scud—Patriot struggle in the Gulf War and the U.S.-Soviet competition in strategic offensive and defensive weaponry and technology provide additional support to Mackinder's sober view of the relative significance of airpower to warfare.

34. See Gray, *op. cit.*; Paul Kennedy, *The Rise and Fall of the Great Powers* (New York: Random Rouse, 1987); Zbigniew Brzezinski, *Game Plan* (New York: The Atlantic Monthly Press, 1986).
35. Gray, *op. cit.*, p. 4.
36. Mackinder, *Democratic Ideals and Reality*, pp. 262, 264.
37. Ibid., p. 155.

4

The First Cold Warrior

During the early post-Second World War years, James Burnham, a leading American Trotskyite in the 1930s, emerged as a chief critic of the policy of containment as theorized by the State Department's Policy Planning Chief, George F. Kennan and implemented by the Truman administration. At this time, Burnham was a prominent liberal anticommunist associated with the journal *Partisan Review* who had worked for the Office of Strategic Services during the war. In three books written between 1947 and 1952, and in hundreds of articles written over a twenty-three-year period for the conservative magazine *National Review*, Burnham criticized containment from the ideological Right, arguing for a more offensive strategy to undermine Soviet power. That strategy, which Burnham called "liberation" and others called "rollback," was widely ridiculed at the time and subsequently, even though, ironically, Kennan in his memoirs called it "persuasive."[1] Decades later, however, the Reagan administration's confrontational style and offense-oriented policies during the 1980s, an approach which arguably resulted in the collapse of the Soviet Empire and the end of the Cold War, can be said to have vindicated Burnham's strategic views.

Burnham was born in Chicago in 1905. His father, Claude George Burnham, who emigrated as a child to the United States from England, was an executive with the Burlington Railroad. James attended Princeton University where he studied English literature and philosophy, and graduated first in his class, delivering his valedictory address in Latin. Burnham earned a masters degree at Balliol College, Oxford University, in 1929; later that year he accepted a teaching position in the philosophy department of New York University. He remained on the faculty of NYU until 1953.

From 1930-1933, Burnham co-edited (with Philip Wheelwright) *Symposium*, a review devoted to literary and philosophical criticism. In 1932, he and Wheelwright wrote a textbook entitled *Introduction to Philosophical Analysis*. During his editorship of *Symposium*, Burnham became acquainted with Sidney Hook, a colleague in the Philosophy Department at NYU. According to Hook, their relationship became "quite friendly" when *Symposium* published Hook's essay "Toward the Understanding of Karl Marx." Burnham's articles in *Symposium* impressed Hook and other readers, including Soviet exile Leon Trotsky.

During the 1930s, with the country in the throes of a great economic depression, Burnham gradually joined the Trotskyist wing of the international communist movement. He had read Marx and Engels while living in France in 1930, and was later greatly impressed by Trotsky's *History of the Russian Revolution*. His move to the far left, however, was not without detours along the way. For example, in the April 1933 issue of *Symposium*, Burnham described the Communist Party as "ridiculously utopian" and "barbaric." John P. Diggins, one of Burnham's biographers, believes that three principal factors persuaded Burnham to join the communist movement: an article by Sidney Hook on Marx; Adolf Berle's and Gardiner Means's book, *The Modern Corporation and Private Property*; and Burnham's tour of the country in the summer of 1933 where, in Diggin's words, "he encountered the first stirrings of an authentic class struggle."

In 1933, Burnham helped Hook, A.J. Muste, and J. B. S. Hardman organize the American Workers Party. The next year, that Party merged with the Trotskyite Communist League of America to form the Socialist Workers Party. Burnham, according to Hook, emerged as the Party's most admired and "most distinguished intellectual figure." Samuel Francis, another Burnham biographer, notes that during that time Burnham was considered a "leading spokesman" of the Trotskyite branch of the international communist movement. Diggins goes further, describing Burnham as Trotsky's "chief spokesman" within American intellectual circles. Burnham became an editor of the Party's monthly journal, *New International*, wherein he defended Trotsky from Stalinist verbal attacks. Initially, Burnham viewed Stalinism as an "aberration of Bolshevism." He saw Trotsky as Lenin's true heir, and Trotskyism as the fulfillment of the ideals of the Bolshevik Revolution. After the signing of the Nazi-Soviet Non-

Aggression Pact in August 1939, however, Burnham began distancing himself from Trotsky (who defended the pact). In May 1940 Burnham resigned from the Socialist Workers Party, ended his involvement in the international communist movement, and began to write regularly for *Partisan Review*, the leading journal of the noncommunist left.[2]

Burnham emerged as a Cold War strategist in 1944 upon writing an analysis of Soviet postwar goals for the U. S. Office of Strategic Services. The seeds of his intellectual evolution from Trotskyist to anticommunist cold warrior were planted during the time period between his break with communism and the beginning of the Cold War. It was then that Burnham formulated his "science of politics" and began viewing the world through a geopolitical prism. This intellectual evolution began in 1941 with the publication of his *The Managerial Revolution*, a study in which he theorized that the world was witnessing the emergence of a new ruling class, "the managers," who would soon replace the rule of capitalists and communists alike. The book was an instant best-seller and was translated into most major foreign languages. It received critical acclaim from the *New York Times*, *Time*, the *New Leader*, *Saturday Review* and leading opinion-makers of the day. John Kenneth Galbraith recalled that *The Managerial Revolution* was "widely read and discussed" among policymakers in Washington in 1941.[3] William Barrett remembered it as "an original and brilliant book when it appeared" which "anticipated by a good number of years the discovery of the 'New Class.'"[4]

The Managerial Revolution is mostly remembered as a political and socioeconomic work, which in part it was. What is often overlooked, or at least understated, is that the study was Burnham's first intellectual foray into global geopolitics. In it he sketched an emerging postwar world divided into "three strategic centers for world control": (1) the northern two-thirds of the Western Hemisphere; (2) North-Central Europe, West Asia and Northern Africa; and (3) the "Asiatic center," East Asia and the offshore islands. "Geography," he explained, "gives certain advantages to each of the contestants in certain areas: to the United States in the northern two-thirds of the two Americas; to the European center in Europe, the northern half of Africa and western Asia; to the Asiatic center in most of the rest of Asia and the islands nearby."

A key factor that conditioned Burnham's selection of those regions as "strategic centers" was their concentrations of modern industry. Burnham predicted that "the world political system will coalesce into three primary super-states, each based upon one of these three areas of advanced industry," and the "nuclei of these three super-states are... Japan, Germany and the United States." Russia, he believed, would break up as a result of the war, "with the western half gravitating toward the European base and the eastern toward the Asiatic." Somewhat more presciently, he predicted the dissolution of the British Empire resulting from "the consolidation of the European Continent." Burnham explained that England's dominant position depended on its ability to "balance Continental nations against each other," and that "the balance of power on the Continent is possible only when the Continent is divided up into a number of genuinely sovereign and powerful states."

Burnham was right, of course, about the collapse of British power, but wrong about its cause. The British Empire broke up because after the war Britain lacked the resources and, more importantly, the will to maintain it. The whole European Continent was not consolidated as Burnham had predicted; instead, the Continent was strategically divided between two super-states. Burnham was correct in predicting that the war would produce a world struggle for power among "super-states." Whereas he foresaw the emergence of three super-states, however, the war's outcome produced only two, the United States and the Soviet Union. Instead of three "strategic centers," there were only two— the northern two- thirds of the Americas and the Asiatic center.

Although in *The Managerial Revolution* Burnham clearly underrated the staying power of the Soviet regime, he accurately forecast the role of the United States in the postwar world. "The United States," he wrote, "constitutes naturally the nucleus of one of the great super-states of the future. From her continental base, the United States is called on to make a bid for maximum world power as against the super-states to be based on the other...central areas." He even foresaw that the United States would become "the 'receiver' for the disintegrating British Empire."[5]

By this time Burnham's break with communism was complete. In *The Managerial Revolution* he noted that "all evidence indicates that the tyranny of the Russian regime is the most extreme that has ever existed in human history, not excepting the regime of Hitler." He no longer believed, as he had in his Trotskyite days, that Stalinism was an aberration from true Marxism-Leninism. "Stalinism," he wrote, " is what Leninism developed into…without any sharp break in the process of development."[6]

In 1943, to his growing anti-communism and geopolitical worldview, Burnham added a "science of politics" based on the ideas and concepts of thinkers that he called "the Machiavellians." The Machiavellians, according to Burnham, studied and analyzed politics in an objective, dispassionate manner in an effort to arrive at certain fundamental truths about "political man." From the writings of Niccolo Machiavelli, Gaetano Mosca, Georges Sorel, Robert Michels, and Vilfredo Pareto, Burnham learned that: (1) all politics is concerned with the struggle for power among individuals and groups; (2) genuine political analysis involves correlating facts and formulating hypotheses about the future without reference to what ought to happen; (3) there is a distinction between the "formal" and "real" meaning of political rhetoric which can only be discovered by analyzing the rhetoric in the context of the actual world of time, space and history; (4) "political man" is primarily a "non-logical" actor driven by "instinct, impulse and interest"; (5) rulers and political elites are primarily concerned with maintaining and expanding their power and privileges; (6) rulers and elites hold power by "force and fraud"; (7) all governments are sustained by "political formulas" or myths; (8) all societies are divided into a "ruling class" and the ruled; and (9) in all societies the "structure and composition" of the ruling class changes over time.[7]

The Machiavellians is the most complete exposition of Burnham's approach to the study and analysis of politics. Samuel Francis judges it to be "Burnham's most important book," and opines that "virtually all of Burnham's writing since *The Machiavellians* must be understood in reference to it."[8] Brian Crozier agrees, calling *The Machiavellians* "the most fundamental of Burnham's books," and "the key to everything he wrote subsequently."[9] Joseph Sobran calls the book "the key to Burnham's thought."[10] John B. Judis believes that Burnham's approach to analyzing power politics as set forth in *The Machiavellians*, "informed his tactical understanding of the Cold War."[11]

In the spring of 1944, a year after writing *The Machiavellians* and just three years after *The Managerial Revolution*, Burnham used his "science of politics," his understanding of the nature of Soviet communism, and his grasp of global geopolitical realities to prepare an analysis of Soviet postwar goals for the Office of Strategic Services

(OSS).[12] Although there is some lack of clarity on just when it was written, according to Diggins and Christopher Hitchens, Burnham's analysis was prepared for the U.S. delegation to the Yalta Conference. His study of Soviet intentions was later incorporated into his first Cold War book, *The Struggle for the World* (1947). As Burnham noted in the opening essay of *The War We Are In*, "The analysis of communist and Soviet intentions in Part I of *The Struggle for the World* was originally part of a secret study prepared for the Office of Strategic Services in the spring of 1944 and distributed at that time to the relevant Washington desks."[13] In his OSS paper, *The Struggle for the World* and in two essays that appeared in the spring of 1944 and early 1945 in *Partisan Review*, Burnham warned that the Soviet Union was aiming at no less than domination of the Eurasian landmass. He identified the communist-inspired mutiny in the Greek Navy at Alexandria in April 1944 as the beginning of what he called the "Third World War." The mutiny was quickly crushed by the British, but Burnham saw larger forces at work. The mutineers were members of the ELAS, the military wing of the Greek Communist Party-controlled EAM, which, in turn, was directed by the Soviet Union. The incident, therefore, was fundamentally a clash between Britain and the Soviet Union, at the time ostensibly allies in the still-raging Second World War. To Burnham, this meant that the Greek mutiny was a skirmish in another and different war. Events in China, too, indicated to him that supposed allies in the war against Japan— Chiang Kai-shek's army and the communist Chinese forces led by Mao Tse-tung—were battling each other as much or more than they were opposing Japanese forces. From these events he concluded that "the armed skirmishes of a new war have started before the old war is finished."[14]

The new phase of Soviet policy evidenced by Greek and Chinese events, according to Burnham, was the sixth major period in Soviet policy since 1917. The first period, "War Communism," lasted from 1918 to 1921. It was succeeded by the New Economic Policy (NEP) which continued until 1928. The years 1928 to 1935 marked the "Third Period" which encompassed the first Five Year Plans and the forced collectivization of agriculture. The fourth period, which Burnham called the "Popular Front," lasted the next four years, and was followed by the "Hitler Pact," from 1939-1941. After an "interregnum" between 1941 and 1943 when the very survival of the regime was at stake, the sixth or "Tehran" period commenced. Writing in the spring of 1944, Burnham concluded that "the object of the present (Tehran) period is to end the European phase of the war on a basis favorable to the perspectives of the Soviet ruling class: that is, in *de facto* Stalinist domination of the Continent."[15]

Burnham believed Stalin's foreign policy was driven by a "geopolitical vision" that corresponded to the theories and concepts of the great British geographer, Sir Halford Mackinder.[16] "Out of this war," explained Burnham, "Stalin has translated into realistic political perspective the dream of theoretical geopolitics: domination of Eurasia." Borrowing Mackinder's terminology, Burnham warned that, "Starting from...the Eurasian heartland, the Soviet power...flows outward, west into Europe, south into the Near East, east into China, already lapping the shores of the Atlantic, the Yellow and China seas, the Mediterranean, and the Persian Gulf...."[17] The goals of Soviet foreign policy as he saw them were: (1) the political consolidation of Eurasia under Soviet control; (2) the weakening of all noncommunist governments; and (3) a Soviet-controlled world empire.

Burnham's OSS study perceptively identified the postwar geopolitical structure that was then emerging from the ashes of the Second World War. It did so a full two years before George Kennan wrote his "Long Telegram" from Moscow and Winston Churchill delivered his "Iron Curtain" speech in Fulton, Missouri. It even predated Kennan's lesser-known papers, "Russia—Seven Years Later" (September 1944) and "Russia's International Position At the Close of the War With Germany" (May 1945), which predicted future difficulties between the United States and Soviet Union. No one foresaw or recognized the emergence of the Cold War more accurately, more comprehensively, or earlier than James Burnham.[18]

Burnham's work for the OSS marked a turning point in his intellectual career. His first two books written after his break with Trotskyism were broad sociopolitical works, concerned more with political trends within countries than geopolitical conflicts between countries. After the OSS study and for the rest of his career, however, with two major exceptions he brought his intellectual gifts to bear almost exclusively upon the central geopolitical struggle of the second half of the twentieth century, the Cold War.

"The Sixth Turn of the Communist Screw" and "Lenin's Heir," which appeared in *Partisan Review* in the summer of 1944 and early 1945, respectively, were the first *public* indications of Burnham's altered focus (the OSS study remained secret). The Soviet Union, he asserted, was positioned to extend its political control from the Heart-land to the remaining key power centers of the Eurasian Continent. Moreover, Soviet goals would not likely change after Stalin since Stalinism was "a triumphant application" of Leninism. "There is nothing basic that Stalin has done... from the institution of terror as the primary foundation of the state to the assertion of a political monopoly, the seeds and even the shoots of which were not planted and flourishing under Lenin." "Stalin," wrote Burnham, "is Lenin's Heir. Stalinism is communism."[19] Burnham's linking of Stalin to Lenin produced, according to the historian Richard H. Pells, "a painful reexamination of socialist doctrine among American intellectuals in the immediate postwar years."[20] Many on the anti-Stalinist Left still believed that Stalinism had betrayed, not fulfilled Leninism. As William Barrett recalled, "Hitherto, the name of Lenin had been protected almost as a holy relic; the blame for any miscarriage of the Russian Revolution had been shunted over entirely on the head of Stalin, who thus provided a ready-made excuse for not locating the fault within the nature of Marxist doctrine itself."[21] Most of the anti-Stalinist Left, however, was not ready to so drastically and fundamentally change the premises of their political beliefs.

Any lingering doubts in the intellectual community about James Burnham's shifting intellectual focus were dispelled by the publication in 1947 of *The Struggle for the World*. There, for the first time in the United States and the West, was a broad, comprehensive analysis of the beginning of the Cold War, the nature of the Soviet communist threat to the world, and a strategy for U.S. and Western victory. Over the next five years, Burnham expanded and refined his analysis in two more books, *The Coming Defeat of Communism* (1950) and *Containment or Liberation?* (1952). Those books present a penetrating and lucid trilogy on the early years of the Cold War. Burnham's admirers, such as Brian Crozier, Samuel Francis, and John O'Sullivan, have treated the three books as essentially one three-volume work. O'Sullivan, in a brilliant, reflective essay in *National Review*, demonstrated that the fundamental geopolitical vision informing Burnham's Cold War trilogy is traceable to *The Managerial Revolution*.

These three works by Burnham span the time period from 1944 to 1952, and can be analytically divided into three broadly defined topics: (1) the global context of the struggle and the nature of the Soviet communist threat; (2) estimates and critiques of then existing

U.S. and Western policies for dealing with the threat; and (3) proposals or strategies to effectively respond to the threat and achieve ultimate victory. Each book of the trilogy discusses, with varying emphases, those three topics; when considered together, they show Burnham's ability to respond to specific events and changes within a larger, consistent intellectual framework.

All three books also manifest the continued influence on Burnham's thought of "the Machiavellians" and the geopolitical theorist Halford Mackinder. He described the Soviet Union of 1945 as controlling the vast interior of Eurasia that Mackinder termed the Heartland of the "World-Island" (the Eurasian-African landmass). The Soviet position, wrote Burnham, "is...the strongest possible position on earth." "[T]here is no geographical position on earth which can in any way be compared with [the Soviet] main base."[22] The Heartland, he explained, is "the most favorable strategic position of the world."[23] From its Heartland base, the Soviet Union was positioned to expand into Europe, the Middle East, and Eastern and Southern Asia.

The United States and North America, according to Burnham (and here he borrowed from both Mackinder and Yale University's Nicholas Spykman), constitute "an island lying off the shores of the great Eurasian landmass."[24] Geopolitically, the United States was to Eurasia what Britain was to Europe—an island facing a great continental landmass. Both Mackinder and Spykman made this precise analogy. (Spykman judged the power potential of coastal Eurasia — Europe, the Middle East, and East Asia which he termed the "Rimland"— to be greater than that of the Heartland).[25] Burnham agreed with Mackinder that "potentially, the Heartland controls the Eurasian landmass as a whole, and, for that matter, the...African Continent." It was "an axiom of geopolitics," Burnham explained, "that if any one power succeeded in organizing the Heartland and its outer barriers, that power would be certain to control the world." (Mackinder had written in 1919 that control of the Heartland and command of the World-Island would lead to world dominance). Air power and atomic weapons, Burnham believed, "upset the certainty of this...axiom," but the "facts of geography" still gave the Soviet Union an incomparable advantage in the post war struggle because "[g]eographically, strategically Eurasia encircles America, overwhelms it."[26]

Burnham pictured the Soviet geopolitical position as a "set of concentric rings around an inner circle."[27] (Mackinder's 1904 world map consisted of the Russian-occupied heartland or "pivot state" bordered by an "inner or marginal crescent" and far removed from an "outer or insular crescent"). Burnham's inner circle was the Soviet Union. The first concentric ring contained the Kuriles, South Sakhalin Island, Mongolia, Turkish regions, Bessarabia and Bukovina, Moldavia, Ukraine, East Poland, East Prussia, the Baltic States, and Finnish regions—territories already absorbed or soon to be absorbed by Soviet power. The second ring included Korea, Manchuria, north China, the Middle East, the Balkans, Austria, Germany, Poland, Scandinavia, and Finland—territories within range of Soviet domination. The third ring contained central and southern China, Italy, France, smaller Western European states, and Latin America—areas where Soviet influence or neutralization was possible. The fourth and final circle included England and the British Commonwealth and the United States and its dependencies—territories forming the rival base of global power.

This geographical setting formed the surroundings for a clash between two major power centers or, as Burnham referred to them in *The Managerial Revolution*, super-states. The clash, according to Burnham, proceeded "simultaneously and integrally along political, economic, ideological, sociological and military lines."[28] It "affects and is affected by events in all parts of the earth, " opined Burnham, and was zero-sum in nature.[29] A U.S. or Western defeat was a Soviet or communist gain, and vice versa.

The Soviet enemy, wrote Burnham, was the head of "a worldwide conspiratorial movement for the conquest of a monopoly of power."[30] Conspiracy, deception, and terror were integral and essential aspects of Soviet communism. Soviet leaders and their clients conducted "a political, subversive, ideological, religious, economic,...guerilla, sabotage war, as well as a war of open arms" against the West.[31] The communists exerted external pressure on target countries and sought to infiltrate those countries' trade union movements, technical and scientific establishments and media enterprises. The ultimate goal of Soviet policy, as manifested in official documents, speeches and a plethora of Soviet actions since 1944, was "the conquest of the world."[32]

The United States from 1945 to 1952, as we know, reacted to this global challenge by gradually positioning itself in opposition to Soviet encroachments. Thus emerged the policy of containment which was explained most succinctly by George F. Kennan, the State

Department's Policy Planning Chief, in his famous "X" article in the July 1947 issue of *Foreign Affairs*. Even before Kennan's highly influential article appeared, Burnham accurately perceived the broad contours and direction of early post-war American foreign policy. In *The Struggle for the World*, Burnham noted that during the latter stages of the Second World War, U.S. policy amounted to "appeasement" of her wartime Soviet ally. The United States ceded to the Soviets the Kurile Islands, South Sakhalin Island, Darien, Port Arthur, Manchuria, northern Korea, Yugoslavia, Czechoslavakia, eastern Germany, and part of Austria, all in an effort to "get along" with Russia. The United States coerced Chiang Kai-shek into joining a coalition government with the communists in China, "when we should have aided Chiang," Burnham wrote, "to block communist domination of...the Eastern Coastland of Eurasia."[33] United States policy, Burnham lamented, "has not hindered but furthered communist expansion on Eurasia; it has not combatted but aided communist infiltration all over the world." Those policy failures, he believed, resulted from "a completely false estimate of communism and...of the communist dominated Soviet Union." American statesmen mistakenly believed that Soviet Russia was a normal, traditional nation-state, and that Soviet leaders could be influenced by demonstrations of good intentions by the United States. Those flawed judgments and beliefs, Burnham thought, resulted from even more fundamental U.S. handicaps: political immaturity and ineptness; a provincialism and ignorance of world affairs; a misconception about human nature; and a tendency toward "abstract, empty and sentimental...idealism." Judging by the evidence of its policies up to 1946, Burnham believed that it was "unlikely that the United states will adopt any sustained, consistent, long-term world policy," but instead will follow a "policy of vacillation."[34]

Burnham's view of U.S. policy became somewhat more optimistic when the Truman administration moved forcefully to block Soviet threats to Iran, Turkey, Greece, Berlin, and Italy, and Tito moved Yugoslavia out of the Soviet orbit. In *The Coming Defeat of Communism*, he wrote that "Our general diplomacy and foreign policy could be judged, compared to our past performances, reasonably strong and intelligent."[35] He applauded what he viewed as a shift in policy from appeasement to containment. But he viewed containment favorably only as a temporary defensive policy to block communist expansion. As a long term policy, containment, wrote Burnham, was incapable of achieving victory in the Cold War. He identified four principal defects in the policy: (1) it was not "sufficiently unified," that is, it was not being applied consistently by all U.S. policymakers and agencies; (2) it was too narrow in that it overemphasized the military aspect of the struggle to the detriment of the political, economic, ideological, and sociological aspects; (3) it was wholly defensive in nature; and (4) it lacked an objective, that is, it did not seek the "destruction of communist power."

The most serious defect of containment, according to Burnham, was the policy's defensive nature. This criticism appeared in all three books of Burnham's Cold War trilogy, and it was the major theme of *Containment or Liberation?* (1952). A "defensive strategy, because it is negative, is never enough," he wrote. It left unsolved the "intolerable unbalance of world political forces."[36] Containment, he explained, "leaves the timing to the communists. They have the initiative; we react....Our policy, as a consequence, is subordinated to, determined by, theirs.... They select the issues, the field, and even the mood of combat."[37] "Containment doesn't threaten anyone," Burnham explained, "it doesn't ask anyone to give up what he's already got."[38] Furthermore, wrote Burnham, the effort to contain communism "is as futile as to try to stop a lawn from getting wet by mopping up each drop from a rotating sprinkler.... [T]o stop the flow we must get at the source."[39]

Even if containment could be successfully implemented by the United States, which Burnham doubted, it would not prevent a Soviet victory in the Cold War. "If the communists succeed in consolidating what they have already conquered," he explained, "then their complete world victory is certain." "The threat," he wrote further, "does not come only from what the communists may do, but from what they have done.... The simple terrible fact is that if things go on as they are now, if for the time being they merely stabilize, then we have already lost."[40] Here Burnham was simply taking Mackinder's geopolitical theories to their logical conclusion. At the time Burnham wrote those lines, the Soviet Empire and its allies controlled the Heartland, Eastern and part of Central Europe, China, northern Korea and parts of Indochina. Political consolidation of such a base, coupled with effective organization of that base's manpower and resources, would give the Soviets command of Mackinder's World Island.[41] "That is why," warned Burnham, "the policy of containment, even if 100% successful, is a formula for Soviet victory."[42]

The Truman administration's focus on Western Europe and the Republican Party's advocacy of what he called an "Asian-American strategy" were both misguided, according to Burnham, because they excluded efforts to penetrate the Soviet sphere. No positive gains could result from those wholly defensive strategies. At most they would buy us some time until the Soviets completed their consolidation and organization of their great continental base, after which, to borrow Mackinder's phrase, "the end would be fated." Burnham's strategic vision, however, consisted of more than simply a critique of the policy of containment. He also set forth in some detail an alternative grand strategy that he called "the policy of liberation." That policy, wrote Burnham in *The Struggle for the World*, must seek to "penetrate the communist fortress," to "reverse the direction of the thrust from the Heartland," to "undermine communist power in East Europe, northern Iran, Afghanistan, Manchuria, northern Korea and China." The United States should seek to exploit Soviet economic and cultural weaknesses. The Western powers should launch a worldwide propaganda offensive against the communist powers. As a result, predicted Burnham, "the communists will be thrown back on the political defensive.,..The walls of their strategic Eurasian fortress...would begin to crumble. The internal Soviet difficulties, economic and social, would be fed a rich medium in which to multiply."[43]

Burnham became more forceful and specific in his policy proposals three years later in *The Coming Defeat of Communism* (1950). He called for America to adopt a policy of "offensive political-subversive warfare" against the Soviet Empire. America should aim, he advised, to increase Soviet economic troubles; to stimulate discontent among the Soviet masses; to encourage more Tito-like defections from the Soviet orbit; to facilitate the "resistance spirit" of the enslaved satellite nations of the empire; to foment divisions within the Soviet elite; and to recruit from behind the Iron Curtain "cadres of liberation."

He was too much of a realist, however, to expect the complete achievement of every U.S. and Western goal in the struggle against communism. In a remarkable chapter in this volume entitled "A Deal With Russia," Burnham set forth five specific conditions that would allow the United States to claim victory in the Cold War without militarily defeating the Soviets: (1) an end to the worldwide communist subversive apparatus; (2) an end to the worldwide Soviet propaganda offensive; (3) the withdrawal of the Soviet army and security services to the pre-1939 Soviet borders; (4) full sovereignty for those territories conquered or annexed by the Soviets since 1939; and (5) the modification of the Soviet governmental structure to permit unrestricted travel, a free press and international inspection of scientific-military facilities.[44] Half a century later, most of Burnham's conditions for victory either are in place or in the process of being achieved.

In *Containment or Liberation?* (1952), Burnham identified Eastern Europe as the crucial target of U.S. strategy. U.S. policy, he wrote, must shift its focus from protecting Western Europe to liberating Eastern Europe. "A strategy which had Eastern Europe as its geopolitical focus—Europe from the Iron Curtain to the Urals—would best serve the American objective," he explained.[45] Eastern Europe, he repeatedly asserted, was the key to the world struggle. Here, again, we see the influence of Mackinder. In his 1919 classic, *Democratic Ideals and Reality*, Mackinder, too, emphasized the importance of preventing a single power from controlling both Eastern Europe and the Heartland. In perhaps the book's most famous passage, Mackinder recommended that an "airy cherub" should whisper to British statesmen the following warning:

> Who rules East Europe commands the Heartland:
>
> Who rules the Heartland commands the World-Island:
>
> Who rules the World-Island commands the World.[46]

When Burnham was writing *Containment or Liberation?*, the Soviet Union controlled the Heartland, Eastern Europe, and was allied to China. Mackinder's geopolitical nightmare was a fact of international life. From Mackinder's 1919 analysis, it logically followed that the only way to prevent Soviet world hegemony was to undermine Soviet positions in Eastern Europe. That is precisely what Burnham's proposed policy of liberation was designed to do.

Two influential statesmen who agreed with the thrust of Burnham's strategy, at least initially during the early years of the Cold War, were John Foster Dulles, who became President Eisenhower's secretary of state, and, ironically, George Kennan, the author of the containment doctrine. Dulles, both before and during the early years of the Eisenhower administration, promoted a policy to "rollback" the Soviet Empire.

Kennan, according to Peter Grose in a new book titled *Operation Rollback*, secretly proposed during the Truman Administration an ambitious program of organized political warfare against the Soviets, which included sabotage and subversion operations, propaganda, and help to resistance forces throughout the Soviet Empire.[47] Kennan's flirtation with a liberation policy ended, according to Grose, when the Truman administration's attempts to implement the strategy failed. Dulles abandoned "rollback" after U.S. responses to the East German, Polish, and Hungarian uprisings in the mid-1950s demonstrated to the world America's unwillingness to support resistance forces within the communist bloc. There is no evidence that either Kennan or Dulles was directly influenced by Burnham's ideas; given his prominence at the time in intellectual circles and his connections with the intelligence community, it is likely that both Kennan and Dulles were familiar with his writings.

Public reaction to Burnham's Cold War trilogy was mixed. Henry Luce gave *The Struggle for the World* prominent play in *Time* and *Life*. Luce even urged President Truman's aide, Charles Ross, to persuade the president to read it.[48] The *Christian Century* speculated that *The Struggle for the World* was the intellectual foundation for the Truman Doctrine announced during the same week that Burnham's book was published. The *American Mercury* published excerpts from all three books. Liberal anticommunist reviewers, such as Arthur Schlesinger, Jr., accepted Burnham's analysis of the Soviet threat but dissented from his call for an offensive policy. For conservative anti-communists, however, Burnham's Cold War trilogy achieved almost biblical status. As George Nash pointed out in his study of the American conservative movement, "More than any other single person, Burnham supplied the conservative intellectual movement with the theoretical formulation for victory in the cold war."[49]

Other reviewers were less kind. Charles Clayton Morrison called *The Struggle for the World* a "blueprint for destruction." Harry Elmer Barnes called it a "most dangerous and un-American book." George Soule in the *New Republic* asserted that Burnham wanted "reaction abroad and repression at home." George Orwell accused Burnham of worshipping power.[50] *The Coming Defeat of Communism* received strong criticism from, among others, James Reston, David Spitz, R.H.S. Crossman, and Louis Fischer. *Containment or Liberation?* received even harsher treatment. The editors of *Foreign Affairs* commented that Burnham's "temper at times outruns his argument."

The *Atlantic Monthly* described the book as "permeated with absolutist thinking." Arthur Schlesinger, Jr. called the book a "careless and hasty job, filled with confusion, contradictions, ignorance and misrepresentation." It was, wrote Schlesinger, "an absurd book by an absurd man."[51]

Burnham's relations with his colleagues on the non-communist Left suffered as a result of his Cold War trilogy. Where once there was widespread acclaim for *The Managerial Revolution*, now his colleagues on the Left disdained him as a warmonger who advocated atomic war. For many liberals (and some conservatives) Burnham's geopolitical vision was too sweeping and apocalyptic. To many, a policy of "liberation" was simply too dangerous in the nuclear age. The non-communist Left sought, at most, to contain the Soviet Union while searching for areas of accommodation. Burnham did not think that accommodation with communism was a long-term possibility. For Burnham, the Cold War was a systemic conflict that would only end when one or the other system changed or was defeated.

Burnham's final and lasting break with the non-communist Left, however, resulted not from his proposed strategy of "liberation," but from his views toward domestic communism and what came to be known as "McCarthyism." Burnham, unlike many intellectuals of the time, believed the testimony of Whittaker Chambers, Elizabeth Bentley, and other ex-communists who identified and described the activities of a Soviet espionage apparatus that operated in the United States during the 1930s and 1940s. He supported the congressional investigations of domestic communism and even testified before investigating committees. He also called for outlawing the Communist Party of the United States.

As Senator Joseph McCarthy became increasingly reckless in his accusations of communist infiltration of government agencies, including the military, the non-communist Left condemned the very idea of loyalty oaths and congressional investigations of American citizens and their ideological affiliations. This was too much for Burnham. Condemning specific erroneous accusations by Senator McCarthy was one thing, but ignoring the reality of communist penetration of the government was potentially suicidal.

Burnham broke with *Partisan Review* and the American Committee for Cultural Freedom (an organization of anticommunist intellectuals) over this issue. He began writing for the *Freeman*, a conservative journal of opinion. In 1954, with his wife's help, he wrote an analysis of communist penetration of the government entitled *The Web of Subversion*.[52] That book, based largely on testimony before congressional committees and the revelations of Chambers, Bentley, and other ex-communists, makes interesting reading today in light of the "Venona project" disclosures which support many of the charges of communist infiltration and subversion that were made in the late 1940s and early 1950s.

In addition to writing books and articles about the Cold War, Burnham lectured at the National War College, the Naval War College, the School for Advanced International Studies and the Air War College. He did consulting work for the Central Intelligence Agency and is reputed to have had a hand in the successful plan to overthrow Mohammed Mossadegh and install the Shah in power in Iran in the early 1950s.

Having severed ties to the anticommunist Left, Burnham found his permanent intellectual home in the pages of William F. Buckley, Jr.'s *National Review*, where for twenty-three years he provided the magazine's readers with a running commentary on the events and personalities of the Cold War. In his regular column, originally called "The Third World War" and later changed to "The Protracted Conflict," Burnham brought his "encyclopedic mind" to bear on specific events as they occurred, but also fitted those events into the larger global geopolitical context. The extent of his knowledge and learning was formidable. A typical Burnham column would include insightful references to Thucydides, Gibbon, Kant, Hobbes, Rousseau, Marx, Tocqueville, Trotsky, Faulkner, Palmerston, Toynbee, J.F.C. Fuller, Clausewitz, Liddell Hart, Mahan, Sun Tzu, Lincoln, Jefferson, Hamilton, Madison, Churchill, and, of course, Mackinder and the "Machiavellians." Burnham, like all great thinkers, understood that he stood on the shoulders of giants.

Burnham demonstrated in his columns an ability to relate seemingly disparate events within a single strategic framework. He showed, for example, how Soviet moves in Cuba and Latin America might affect Berlin and Western Europe; how our Middle East policy could impact on the solidarity of NATO; how our defeat in Indochina, the loss of U.S. nuclear superiority, the rapid de-colonization in Asia and Africa, the French loss of Algeria, and the British pull-out from Suez and Aden amounted to a general Western global retrenchment, and how the resulting power vacuum could be filled by Soviet expansion. He also showed an ability to view world events from a Soviet or communist perspective. Here, he benefited from his Trotskyite past. Several of his most perceptive columns were written from the perspective of a fictional Soviet intelligence officer. Burnham was yet another example of how ex-communists often make the most intelligent and realistic anti-communists.

He had a tendency in some of his writings to be too schematic in his analysis of world events. Not everything that happened in the world significantly affected the Cold War, but Burnham sometimes gave the impression that it did. He also at times portrayed Soviet leaders as almost perfect strategists who nearly always made flawless political and strategic calculations. He sometimes gave Soviet strategists too much credit for causing or influencing world events. He occasionally overrated the strategic stakes involved in local and regional conflicts. The consequences of some of our defeats in the Cold War were not as catastrophic as Burnham thought they would be. But, unlike many other Western observers, at least he understood that there would be negative consequences to those defeats.

Burnham was frequently controversial. In some columns he suggested using nuclear or chemical weapons in Vietnam. Although not anti-Israel, he favored a more balanced U.S. policy in the Middle East, on one occasion writing that if Americans had to choose between oil and Israel they should choose oil. He heaped scorn upon the "peace movement" in the United States, viewing it as a composition of pro-communists and "useful idiots." However well intentioned a "peacenik" was, thought Burnham, the political and strategic effect of his conduct benefited the nation's enemies. He refused to unambiguously condemn Joe McCarthy and he defended congressional investigations of domestic communists. He viewed the outcome of the Cuban Missile Crisis as a U.S. defeat and a retreat from the Monroe Doctrine. Although he recognized there was a Sino-Soviet dispute and recommended that the United States exploit the differences between the two communist giants, he dismissed the notion that the dispute was ideological, maintaining that both countries were part of the world communist enterprise and, therefore, enemies of the United States. He viewed superpower summits and arms control efforts as dangerous Western illusions. Finally, he used his column to attack liberal icons such as Eleanor Roosevelt, Harry Truman, George Kennan, J. Robert Oppenheimer, and Linus Pauling.

In his *National Review* columns Burnham was not a predictable conservative. He had a soft spot for Robert McNamara, repeatedly defending him from critics on the Left and Right. He criticized libertarian conservatives who opposed the draft and the welfare state, and other conservatives who sought ideological purity in their political candidates. He wrote in opposition to ballistic missile defenses. He advocated ending U.S. control of the Panama Canal and favored granting diplomatic recognition to communist China. He also criticized those conservatives who overestimated the military, technological, and economic prowess of the Soviet Union.

What is most striking about Burnham's *National Review* columns, however, is how often he got things right. Consider Vietnam. As early as March 1962, Burnham predicted a U.S. defeat in Indochina. He criticized Kennedy's policy of confining military activities to South Vietnam. Fighting a war in this manner, he argued, was "senseless butchery." Four months later he criticized the concept of "escalation" warfare, which became a key aspect of America's failed Vietnam policy. In a January 1963 column, he wrote that the nation was losing the war in Vietnam, and he predicted that for Americans the war was "likely to get much dirtier before it is over." That year, he scathingly attacked the "qualitative and quantitative" restrictions on U.S. military activity in Vietnam, and predicted that an unwillingness to attack the enemy's base of operations (North Vietnam) would lead to the United States pulling out of Indochina.

In a September 1964 column, Burnham argued that we had two options in Vietnam: use enough force and an appropriate strategy to win or get out. Two months later Burnham wrote that Lyndon Johnson would be a war president. By 1966, Burnham was criticizing Johnson for wasting American lives by forbidding our troops the use of weapons and methods that could win the war. He also perceived that the North Vietnamese communists viewed the United States, not Indochina, as "the principal front in the war." In a February 1968 piece, Burnham noted that television coverage was negatively impacting the U.S. war effort. A month later, he pronounced the U.S. strategy of "gradual escalation" a failure. By August 1968, Burnham recognized that the domestic political debate over Vietnam was now a debate about "how to get out." In a July 1969 column, Burnham foresaw that the communists would only agree to a "settlement" that guaranteed their takeover of South Vietnam. A year later, he accurately characterized Nixon's "Vietnamization" policy as a "policy of withdrawal." As negotiations intensified and the 1972 election drew nearer, Burnham wrote that the U.S. had effectively lost the war; what Nixon and Kissinger were calling an "honorable peace" was nothing more than a defeat. By April 1972, Burnham predicted that South Vietnam would not survive as an independent nation, and he viewed our failure there as resulting from the "self-imposed strategic prison" of containment. After the peace agreement was signed to much public acclaim, Burnham noted the uncomfortable facts that South Vietnam was encircled and infiltrated by the enemy, and predicted that the U.S. would not muster the political will to intervene again to prevent the now certain communist takeover of the South.[53]

Burnham's prescience in his columns was not limited to Vietnam. He dismissed unsupported claims of Soviet technological superiority in the wake of Sputnik. He criticized Western observers who uncritically accepted Soviet disinformation regarding economic achievements, military power, and technological advances. In September 1962, he correctly guessed that the Soviets had placed nuclear missiles in Cuba. He was an early critic of the "détente" policy with its accompanying emphasis on arms control, summitry, and trade concessions. In the early 1970s, he wrote about the "internationalization of terrorism" and noted the links between the various terrorist groups, anticipating by several years the more detailed analysis of this phenomenon by Claire Sterling in *The Terror Network*. He also anticipated by several years Jeane J. Kirkpatrick's analysis in *Commentary* of the important distinctions between totalitarian and authoritarian regimes. He even foresaw the rise in the United States of an imperial presidency that would upset the delicate constitutional balance established by the Founding Fathers, a topic he discussed at length in his much neglected book, *Congress and the American Tradition* (1959).[54]

The most important thing Burnham got right was a strategy for winning the Cold War. The essence of that strategy was to wage political, psychological, and economic warfare against the Soviet Empire and thereby weaken and eventually break Soviet control over Eastern and Central Europe. The strategy's key elements were the following: (1) an ideological and propaganda offensive against Soviet rule; (2) assisting dissident and resistance groups within the Soviet Empire; (3) using U.S. economic and technological strength to put strains on the vulnerable Soviet economy; (4) utilizing psycho-political warfare to encourage fear and divisions among the Soviet elite;

(5) using trade and other economic weapons to further weaken the Soviet economy; and (6) forcing the Soviets onto the geopolitical defensive.

During the 1980s, as Peter Schweizer, Jay Winik, Andrew Busch, and others have described, the Reagan administration formulated and implemented an offensive geopolitical strategy designed to undermine Soviet power.[55] While there is no evidence that Reagan or his advisers consciously sought to apply Burnham's precise strategy of "liberation," Reagan's strategy consisted of policies that in a fundamental sense were remarkably similar to Burnham's proposals. Reagan launched a vigorous ideological and propaganda offensive against the Soviets, calling Soviet leaders liars and cheats, predicting the Soviets' near-term demise, and daring its leader to tear down the Berlin Wall. Reagan provided aid and encouragement to Poland's Solidarity movement and the Afghan rebels, two resistance movements within the Soviet Empire. Reagan built up U.S. military forces, deployed intermediate range nuclear missiles in Europe, and announced the plan to develop the Strategic Defense Initiative (SDI), thus putting additional pressure on the already strained Soviet economy, thus serving to convince the Soviets that they could not win an arms race with the United States.

The so-called "Reagan Doctrine" placed the Soviets on the geopolitical defensive throughout the world. Less than a year after Reagan left office, the Berlin Wall came down, the enslaved nations of Eastern Europe revolted, and the Soviet Empire was on its way to dissolution. Burnham, it turns out, was right all along. Containment was not enough to win the Cold War. It took an offensive geopolitical strategy to undermine Soviet power. And, as Burnham had argued, Eastern Europe was the key to victory.

Burnham had little confidence that such a strategy as his would ever be implemented by the United States. His pessimism in this regard was most profoundly expressed in his 1964 book, *Suicide of the West*.[56] Burnham argued that since reaching the apex of its power in 1914, Western civilization had been contracting, most obviously in a geographical sense. Burnham described the contraction in terms of "effective political control over acreage." Because the West continued to possess more than sufficient relative economic, political, and military power to maintain its ascendancy, the only explanation for the contraction was an internal lack of will to use that power. Hence, the West was in the process of committing "suicide." In the book he was highly critical of modern liberalism, but the author did not claim, as some have stated, that liberalism caused or was responsible for the West's contraction. "The cause or causes," he wrote, "have something to do...with the decay of religion and with an excess of material luxury; and...with getting tired, worn out as all things temporal do." Liberalism, instead, was "the ideology of Western suicide." It "motivates and justifies the contraction, and reconciles us to it."[57] He expressed his belief that the collapse of the West was probable, although not inevitable. He acknowledged the possibility of a "decisive change" resulting in a reversal of the West's contraction.

Suicide of the West provided a good analysis and explanation of historical events and trends, but its main conclusion is wrong. This is not so because Burnham misunderstood historical events or misjudged current trends; his mistake derived from his apparent unwillingness in this instance to be more open to the possibility that things might change. The Western contraction did stop, at least temporarily. The United States found the will to use its resources and adopt an offensive strategy to win the Cold War.

In 1978 Burnham suffered a stroke from which he never fully recovered. His last column for *National Review* was an analysis of the potential impact of the Egyptian-Israeli Camp David Accord on U.S.-Soviet relations in the Middle East. In 1983, Ronald Reagan, who presided over the West's victory in the Cold War, presented the United States's highest civilian honor, the Presidential Medal of Freedom, to James Burnham, who had envisioned a strategy for that victory nearly forty years before. The citation reads,

> As a scholar, historian and philosopher, James Burnham has profoundly affected the way America views itself and the world. Since the 1930's, Mr. Burnham has shaped the thinking of world leaders. His observations have changed society and his writings have become guiding lights in mankind's quest for truth. Freedom, reason and decency have had few greater champions in this century than James Burnham.

At the end of July 1987, James Burnham died of cancer. Two years later, with the fall of the Berlin Wall, his vision became reality.

Notes

1. George F. Kennan, *Memoirs 1950-1963* (New York: Pantheon Books, 1972), p. 100.
2. The facts and circumstances of Burnham's early life and intellectual activity are derived from: John P. Diggins, *Up From Communism: Conservative Odysseys in*

American Intellectual Development (New York: Columbia University Press, Morningside Edition, 1994), pp. 161-180; Sidney Hook, *Out of Step: An Unquiet Life in the 20th Century* (New York: Carrol & Graf Publishers, Inc., 1988), pp. 192-204; Samuel Francis, *Power and History: The Political Thought of James Burnham* (Lanham, MD.: University Press of America, 1984), p 7; Kevin J. Smant, *How Great the Triumph: James Burnham, Anticommunism and the Conservative Movement* (Lanham, MD: University Press of America, 1992), pp. 1-21; and Sidney Hook, "Radical, Teacher, Technician," *National Review* (September 11, 1987), pp. 32-33.

3.   John Kenneth Galbraith, *National Review* (September 11, 1987), p. 35.

4.   William Barrett, *The Truants: Adventures Among the Intellectuals* (Garden City, NY: Anchor Press/Doubleday, 1982), p. 86.

5.   James Burnham, *The Managerial Revolution: What is Happening in the World* (New York: John Day Company, Inc., 1941), pp. 179, 176, 180, 177, 262, 264.

6.   Burnham, *The Managerial Revolution*, at pp. 47, 195.

7.   James Burnham, *The Machiavellians: Defenders of Freedom* (New York: John Day Company, Inc., 1943), pp. 223-226.

8.   Francis, *Power and History*, p. 49.

9.   Brian Crozier, *National Review* (September 11, 1987), p. 36.

10.   Joseph Sobran, *National Review* (September 11, 1987), p. 46.

11.   John B. Judis, *Grand Illusion: Critics and Champions of the American Century* (New York: Farrar, Straus & Giroux, 1992), p. 155.

12.   Diggins, *Up From Communism*, p. 319; Francis, *Power and History*, p. 67; Judis, *Grand Illusion*, p. 146; Christopher Hitchens, "How Neo-Conservatives Perish," *For the Sake of Argument* (London: Verso, 1993), p. 144; George H. Nash, *The Conservative Intellectual Movement in America Since 1945* (New York: Basic Books, Inc., 1976), p. 92; James Burnham, *The War We Are In: The Last Decade and the Next* (New Rochelle, NY: Arlington House, 1967), p. 10.

13.   Burnham, *The War We Are In*, p. 10.

14.   James Burnham, *The Struggle for the World* (New York: John Day Company, Inc., 1947), p. 3.

15.   James Burnham, "The Sixth Turn of the Communist Screw," *Partisan Review*, Volume 11, Number 3, Summer 1944.

16.   For an exhaustive analysis of Mackinder's writings, see Francis P. Sempa, "Mackinder's World," *American Diplomacy* (Winter 2000) , www.americandiplomacy.org; Francis P. Sempa, "The Geopolitics Man," *National Interest* (Fall 1992), pp. 96-102; and Francis P. Sempa, "Geopolitics and American Strategy: A Reassessment," in Herbert M. Levine and Jean Edward Smith, eds., *The Conduct of American Foreign Policy Debated* (New York: McGraw-Hill Publishing Co., 1990), pp. 330-343.

17.   James Burnham, "Lenin's Heir," *Partisan Review*, Volume 12, 1945, Issue 1, p. 66.

18.   William C. Bullitt appears to have recognized even earlier than Burnham that the U.S. would have postwar problems with the Soviet Union. Bullitt wrote lengthy, prophetic memos to FDR on January 29, 1943 and August 10, 1943 warning the president about Soviet post-war goals. Bullitt also wrote a book in 1946 entitled *The Great Globe Itself* that provided a realistic assessment of Soviet post-war intentions. Burnham's analyses and proposals as set forth in the OSS paper, the *Partisan Review* essays, and his early Cold War trilogy, however, are more comprehensive than Bullitt's works.

19.   Burnham, "Lenin's Heir," pp. 71-72.

20.   Richard H. Pells, *The Liberal Mind in a Conservative Age: American Intellectuals in the 1940s & 1950s* (New York: Harper & Row, 1985), p. 82.

21.   Barrett, *The Truants*, pp. 88-89.

22. Burnham, *The Struggle for the World*, p. 162.

23. James Burnham, *The Coming Defeat of Communism* (New York: John Day Company, Inc., 1950), p. 14.

24. James Burnham, *Containment or Liberation?* (New York: John Day Company, Inc., 1952), p. 147.

25. Nicholas J. Spykman, *The Geography of the Peace* (New York: Harcourt, Brace, 1944).

26. Burnham, *The Struggle for the World*, pp. 114-115.

27. Burnham, *The Struggle for the World*, p. 97.

28. Burnham, *Coming Defeat of Communism*, p. 23.

29. Burnham, *Containment or Liberation?*, p. 73.

30. Burnham, *Struggle for the World*, p. 59.

31. Burnham, *Coming Defeat of Communism*, p. 104.

32. Burnham, *Struggle for the World*, p. 90.

33. Burnham, *Struggle for the World*, p. 171.

34. Burnham, *Struggle for the World*, pp. 163, 159, 10, 239-240.

35. Burnham, *Coming Defeat of Communism*, p.99.

36. Burnham, *Struggle for the World*, p. 181.

37. Burnham, *Coming Defeat of Communism*, p. 100.

38. Burnham, *Containment or Liberation?*, p. 31.

39. Burnham, *Containment or Liberation?*, pp. 36-37.

40. Burnham, *Containment or Liberation?*, pp. 251.

41. Writing three years after Burnham, the great French writer Raymond Aron noted ominously that "Russia has in fact nearly achieved the 'world island' which Mackinder considered the necessary and almost sufficient condition for universal empire." Raymond Aron, *The Century of Total War* (Boston: The Beacon Press, 1955), p. 111.

42. Burnham, *Containment or Liberation?*, p. 251.

43. Burnham, *Struggle for the World*, pp. 162, 197-198, 228-229, 239, 221.

44. Burnham, *Coming Defeat of Communism*, pp. 159-160.

45. Burnham, *Containment or Liberation?*, p. 128.

46. Halford J. Mackinder, *Democratic Ideals and Reality* (New York: W.W. Norton & Company, Inc., 1962), p. 150. The book was originally published in 1919.

47. See John Foster Dulles, "A Policy of Boldness," *Life* (May 19, 1952), pp. 146-160; and Peter Grose, *Operation Rollback: America's Secret War Behind the Iron Curtain* (Boston: Houghton,Mifflin Co., 2000).

48. W. A. Swanberg, *Luce and His Empire* (New York: Charles Scribner's Sons, 1972), p. 254.

49. Nash, *Conservative Intellectual Movement in America*, p. 91.

50. Diggins, *Up From Communism*, p. 322.

51. Smant, *How Great the Triumph*, pp. 36, 43, 51.

52. James Burnham, *The Web of Subversion: Underground Networks in the U.S. Government* (New York: John Day Company, Inc., 1959). It was first published in 1954.

53. "Southeast Asian Contradiction," *National Review* (March 13, 1962), p. 163; "Escalating Downward," in *The War We Are In*, pp. 267-269; "Toujours, la Sale Guerre," *National Review* (January 29, 1963), p. 60; "What Chance in Vietnam," *National Review* (October 8, 1963), p. 304; "The Perils of Under-simplification," *National Review* (September 8, 1964), p. 766; "The Hand on the Trigger," in *The War We Are In*, pp. 95-97; "What is the President Waiting For?," *National Review* (June 28, 1966), p. 612; "Hanoi's Special Weapons System," *National Review* (August 9, 1966), p. 765; "The War in Studio 7," *National Review* (February 27, 1968), p. 179;

"Time for Some Answers," *National Review* (March 26, 1968), p. 282; "An Honorable Peace," *National Review* (July 30, 1968), p. 792; "Front into Government," *National Review* (July 1, 1969), p. 635; "Stripped Down," *National Review* (July 28, 1970), p. 778; "Is It All Over in Vietnam?," *National Review* (April 28, 1972), p. 449; "Peace, Peace but is it Peace?," *National Review* (February 16, 1973), p. 199; "Under Northern Eyes," *National Review* (March 16, 1973), p. 303.

54.   James Burnham, *Congress and the American Tradition* (Chicago: Henry Regnery Company, 1965). First published in 1959.

55.   Peter Schweizer, *Victory: The Reagan Administration's Secret Strategy That Hastened the Collapse of the Soviet Union* (New York: Atlantic Monthly Press, 1994); Jay Winik, *On the Brink: The Dramatic, Behind the Scenes Saga of the Reagan Era and the Men and Women Who Won the Cold War* (New York: Simon & Schuster, 1996); Andrew E. Busch, "Ronald Reagan and the Defeat of the Soviet Empire," *Presidential Studies Quarterly* (Summer 1997), pp. 451-466. The Reagan strategy to undermine Soviet power was laid out in secret National Security Decision Directives in 1982 and 1983 (NSDD-32, NSDD-66 and NSDD-75).

56.   James Burnham, *Suicide of the West: An Essay on the Meaning and Destiny of Liberalism* (Chicago: Regnery Books, 1985). First published in 1964.

57.   Burnham, *Suicide of the West*, pp. 301, 26.

Part 2

Geopolitics from the Cold War to the Twenty-First Century

5

Geopolitics and American Strategy in the Cold War

The dominant goal of U.S. foreign policy from the late 1940s to the end of the Cold War was to contain Soviet power within the geographical boundaries established at the end of World War II. In an absolute sense, the policy of containment failed. Soviet power extended into Southeast Asia and Southwest Asia, Africa, the Middle East, the Caribbean Sea, and Central America. Soviet naval power girded the major bodies of water on the globe. In a more limited sense, however, containment succeeded: the map of Europe was not altered in nearly forty-five years, nor was, in geopolitical terms, the map of Central Asia.

Containing Soviet power was the subject of George F. Kennan's famous 1947 article in *Foreign Affairs,* "The Sources of Soviet Conduct." Kennan argued that, for historical and ideological reasons, the Soviet Union would seek to expand its political control beyond the immediate postwar geographical boundaries. He urged the United States to respond with a policy of "long-term, patient but firm and vigilant containment." He called for "the adroit and vigilant application of counter-force at a series of constantly shifting geographical and political points, corresponding to the shifts and maneuvers of Soviet policy." This policy was not a magnanimous offer to protect the peoples of Europe and Asia from Soviet tyranny: it was based on the central assumption, heightened by two wars, that the security of the United States was ultimately at stake in the balance of power on the Eurasian landmass

Kennan is rightly regarded as the theoretical "father" of containment. Yet, the roots of his concept go back to 1904, when a British geographer delivered a paper to the Royal Geographical Society.

Halford J. Mackinder is known as the founder of modern geopolitics; he might also be called the "grandfather" of the policy of containment.

Mackinder entitled his paper "The Geographical Pivot of History." In it, he drew a geopolitical sketch of the globe, identifying the inner core area of Eurasia as the "pivot area" of world politics. The key characteristics of this "pivot area" were its extensive, continuous flatlands and its inaccessibility to sea power. Reviewing the history of the nomadic invasions of Huns, Avars, Magyars, Khazars, Cumans, Kalmuks, and Mongols, Mackinder wrote, "For a thousand years a series of horse-riding peoples emerged from Asia through the broad interval between the Ural Mountains and the Caspian Sea, rode through the open spaces of southern Russia, and struck home into Hungary in the very heart of the European peninsula."[2]

Particularly revealing were the Mongol invasions, in which "all the settled margins of the Old World sooner or later felt the expansive force of mobile power originating in the steppe. Russia, Persia, India and China were either made tributary, or received Mongol dynasties."[3] Updating history to 1904, Mackinder wrote,

> Russia replaces the Mongol Empire. Her pressure on Finland, on Scandinavia, on Poland, on Turkey, on Persia, on India, and on China replaces the centrifugal raids of the steppe-men. In the world at large she occupies the central strategical position held by Germany in Europe. She can strike on all sides and be struck from all sides, save the north.[4]

Mackinder completed his global sketch by placing the rest of Eurasia outside the pivot area in "a great inner crescent," and putting Britain, Southern Africa, Japan, and North and South America in the "outer crescent." Toward the end of his paper Mackinder issued the following warning: "The oversetting of the balance of power in favor of the pivot state, resulting in its expansion over the marginal lands of Euro-Asia, would permit the use of vast continental resources for fleet-building, and the empire of the world would then be in sight."[5] He suggested three possible contenders for world empire: Germany, Russia and China. Geography offered them this opportunity, but Mackinder pointed out that the power balance was determined by many factors, including "the relative number, virility, equipment and organization of the competing peoples."[6]

Thus, forty-three years before Kennan's article, Mackinder foresaw the rise of a powerful state occupying the "pivot area" and aspiring to global hegemony. After Germany's failed bid for continental domination in World War I, Mackinder greatly expanded on his 1904 ideas. The result, in 1919, was a 200-page tour de force entitled *Democratic Ideals and Reality,* a book that remains the classic work on modern geopolitics. Drawing on his vast knowledge of geography and history, Mackinder analyzed the struggles of ancient Egypt, Greece and Macedonia, the Roman Empire, Europe and the eastern barbarians, and the British Empire. History, according to Mackinder, consisted ultimately of the struggles for power among states and empires. And the key to those struggles could be found in geography.

The uncomfortable reality of the geographical conditions of our planet, according to Mackinder, was that "the grouping of lands and seas, and of fertility and natural pathways, is such as to lend itself to the growth of empires, and in the end of a single world empire."[7] The world consisted of the following geographical elements: one ocean covering nine-twelfths of the globe; one continent covering two-twelfths of the globe; and many smaller islands making up the remaining one-twelfth. The one great continent encompassed Europe, Asia, and Africa; he called this the "World Island." The central strategic position on the World Island was the inner area of Eurasia, previously referred to as the "pivot area," but which Mackinder now called the "Heartland." He described the Heartland as "a great continuous patch in the north and center of the continent. That whole patch, extending right across from the icy, flat shore of Siberia to the torrid, steep coasts of Baluchistan and Persia, has been inaccessible to navigation from the ocean. The opening of it by railways... and by aeroplane routes in the near future, constitutes a revolution in the relations of men to the larger geographical realities of the world."[8] He concluded that it was from this great region that the threat to the rest of the world would emerge.

To grasp more fully Mackinder's grand conception, we must address it in a piecemeal fashion. The first key concept concerns the struggle for power between insular and peninsular powers. Mackinder takes us back to the ancient struggle between peninsular Greece and insular Crete, and describes how a unified Greece (under the Dorians) was able to use the greater resources of the peninsular mainland to conquer Crete; later, however, the Athens-Sparta rivalry "prevented a full exploitation of the peninsula as a sea-base."[9] This same geographical relationship was highlighted in the conquest of (insular) Britain by a united Latin peninsular power, the Roman Empire. Still later, and on a greater scale, a fragmented European peninsula was unable to challenge successfully the sea power base of Britain: France (under Napoleon) and Germany (under Wilhelm II) both failed in this quest.

With this historical-geographical background, Mackinder asks the reader to picture the vast Eurasian-African landmass (the World Island) and North America in a peninsular-insular perspective. "But," he writes, "there is this vital difference, that the world-promontory, when united by modern overland communications, is in fact the World Island, possessed potentially of the advantage both of insularity and of incomparably great resources."[10] Then he poses the ominous questions:

> What if the Great Continent, the whole World Island or a large part of it, were at some future time to become a single and united base of sea-power? Would not the other insular bases be out built as regards ships and out manned as regards seamen? Their fleets would no doubt fight with all the heroism begotten of their histories, but the end would be fated.[11]

The second of Mackinder's key concepts, closely related to the first, relates to the relative advantage of land power over sea power. Sea power, according to Mackinder, is ultimately dependent upon an adequate land base. It was its magnificent land base (in resources and skilled manpower) that made Great Britain a great sea power. But a greater peninsular land base, once united under a single power and free from challenges from another land power, will achieve naval supremacy to defeat the less strongly based insular power. Thus, in Mackinder's strategic conception, a land power that gains control over a large part of the Eurasian-African landmass could harness the vast resources of its land base to constructing the world's most powerful navy and overwhelming all remaining insular powers.

Mackinder's third and most important concept was that of the Heartland. This great, largely unbroken plain of inner Eurasia, inaccessible to sea power, provided its occupant the opportunities to expand in all directions except northward. In 1919 Mackinder included within the Heartland the Black and Baltic Seas, the middle and lower Danube, Asia Minor (Turkey), Armenia, Persia, Tibet, and Mongolia (these were additions to his original concept). He foresaw a "fundamental opposition between East and West Europe"[12]—between the Heartland and the Coastland. Remarkably, in light of ensuing history, he placed the frontier of the East-West struggle in the center of Germany. He explained that the nations of Western Europe "must necessarily be opposed to whatever Power attempts to organize the resources of East Europe and the Heartland.... We [Britain and France] were opposed to the half-German Russian Czardom because Russia was the dominating, threatening force both in East Europe and the Heartland for a century. We were opposed to the wholly German Kaiserdom, because Germany took the lead in East Europe from the Czardom, and would then have crushed the revolting slavs, and dominated East Europe and the Heartland."[13]

Mackinder also recognized that the nations of Western Europe, by themselves, could not counterbalance a single power controlling Eastern Europe and the Heartland: in World War I "West Europe had to call in the help of America, for West Europe alone would not have been able to reverse the decision in the East."[14] It was toward the end of *Democratic Ideals and Reality* that Mackinder issued his famous dictum: "Who rules East Europe commands the Heartland: Who rules the Heartland commands the World Island: Who rules the World Island commands the World."[15] In yet another prophetic comment, he warned the idealists of his time: "No mere scraps of paper, even though they be the written constitution of a League of Nations, are, under the conditions of today, a sufficient guarantee that the Heartland will not again become the center of a world war."[16]

Twenty-two years after the publication of *Democratic Ideals and Reality,* the Heartland and Eastern Europe did indeed become the center of a world war. American memories and perceptions of that conflict tend to focus, quite naturally, on the battles in Western Europe and the Pacific. Yet, the greatest land war in history raged for four years on Germany's eastern front. Hitler's racist notions of Germany's destiny to dominate the Slavic peoples blended well with German geopolitical theories. The German school of *Geopolitik,* headed by Dr. Karl Haushofer, studied and debated the geopolitical theories of Mackinder, Friedrich Ratzel, and Rudolf Kjellen, and adapted Mackinder's conceptions into a blueprint for Eurasian hegemony. Interestingly, Dr. Haushofer advised not only Hitler but also Stalin prior to the German invasion of the Soviet Union.

The war challenged one part of Mackinder's famous dictum: Germany, having conquered Eastern Europe, failed to take command of the Heartland. But the war's outcome brought about Mackinder's geopolitical nightmare: a single power now ruled Eastern Europe and the Heartland.

Was Soviet world hegemony now inevitable? Not necessarily, according to Mackinder's last published work on this topic: a 1943 article in *Foreign Affairs* entitled "The Round World and the Winning of the Peace." In it he contended that his concept of the Heartland" is more valid and useful today than it was either twenty or forty years ago."[17] Further revising the boundaries of the Heartland, he described it roughly in terms of the territory of the Soviet Union. He then warned,

> All things considered, the conclusion is unavoidable that if the Soviet Union emerges from this war as conqueror of Germany, she must rank as the greatest land power on the globe. Moreover, she will be the Power in the strategically strongest defensive position. The Heartland is the greatest natural fortress on earth. For the first time in history it is manned by a garrison sufficient both in number and quality.[18]

Yet, Mackinder now added a feature to his grand conception: the "Midland Ocean." It consisted of three elements: "a bridgehead in France, a moated aerodrome in Britain, and a reserve of trained manpower, agriculture and industries in the eastern United States and Canada."[19] He rated the Midland Ocean as being of "almost equal significance" to the Heartland. He thus foresaw, or prescribed, the North Atlantic Alliance.

Mackinder's ideas were influential in the United States in the immediate postwar years. *Democratic Ideals and Reality* was reprinted in 1942, a year before Mackinder's final article in *Foreign Affairs,* and his conceptions were analyzed and debated. His influence is discernible in some of the foreign policy writings of Walter Lippmann. In *The Century of Total War,* Raymond Aron noted, ominously, that "Russia has in fact nearly achieved the 'world island' which Mackinder considered the necessary and almost sufficient condition for universal empire."[20]

Nicholas Spykman, then Professor of International Relations at Yale University, essentially accepted Mackinder's geographical view of the world, but argued that coastal Eurasia (Mackinder's inner crescent, which Spykman renamed the "Eurasian Rimland"), not the Heartland, was the key to world power. Spykman went so far as to issue a counter-dictum to Mackinder's: "Who controls the rimland rules Eurasia; who rules Eurasia controls the destinies of the world."[21] More will be said about Spykman's ideas below. But Mackinder's influence also was prominent in the writings of Professor Robert Strausz-Hupé and of the Foreign Policy Research Institute he founded at the University of Pennsylvania in the 1950s.

Not all those who were influenced by Mackinder's works saw containment as the most effective strategy for dealing with the Soviet geopolitical threat. In 1944 James Burnham, then working for the Office of Strategic Services, wrote an analysis of the Soviet threat to the West which he later expanded into a book entitled *The Struggle for the World*."[22] In two subsequent volumes, Burnham extended his analysis and advocated policies designed to win what he called the "Third World War."

Burnham adopted Mackinder's geopolitical conception, adding to it an analysis of the revolutionary dimension of Soviet communism. After the communist conquest of China, he urged American policymakers to turn from containment to a policy of "liberation." Viewing China as an appendage of Soviet power (which it essentially was at the time), he argued that the Soviet Union now effectively controlled the bulk of the World Island.

Containment, Burnham contended, was a defeatist policy for two main reasons. First, as a revolutionary ideology, Soviet communism could not be contained behind traditional geographical borders, because the Soviets would expand through political warfare waged by surrogate forces in other countries. Second, Soviet conquests (including China) already gave it command of so much of Eurasia that "if [they] succeed in consolidating what they have already conquered, then their complete world victory is certain....That is why the policy of containment, even if 100 per cent successful, is a formula for Soviet victory."[23]

This is not the place to analyze and critique James Burnham's proposed policy of "liberation" as an alternative to containment. Suffice it to say that his chief contribution to the geopolitical debate was to combine Mackinder's geographical insights with an analysis of the political implications of the Soviet's revolutionary ideology.

Burnham noted, "For the first time in world history, the inner Heartland possessed a mass population, a high level of political organization, and a considerable industralization."[24] He drew a circular map of the world, placing the Soviet Union in the inner circle, coastal Eurasia and Northern Africa in the next circles, and the rest of the world in the outer circles. From its central strategic location, the Soviet Union would, he predicted, exert political pressure on the surrounding areas. Echoing Mackinder, Burnham, in *The Coming Defeat of Communism*, described the Heartland as "the most favorable strategic position of the world."[25] And in *Containment or Lib-*

eration?, he echoed Spykman in describing the geopolitical position of the United States: "Geographically, America, as an off-shore island, has much the same relation to Eurasia as Britain to Europe."[26] He then warned,

> A balance of power does not now exist on the Eurasian continent. On the contrary, there is domination or potential domination by the single Soviet system. That this is true become obvious if we assume the power influence of the United States to be withdrawn from Eurasia. At once, probably without fighting, all of the Eurasian nations still outside of the Soviet Empire would have to submit to Soviet control.[27]

To these geopolitical concepts Burnham added his analysis of what he called the "communist conduct of contemporary war." He believed that Soviet offensive moves would most often take the form of proxy warfare: "The Soviet power has the advantage of fighting in such a way through auxiliary forces during what the rest of the world regards as peacetime, a time therefore when the opponent feels inhibited from taking adequate countermeasures."[28] Furthermore, the Soviets divide the world into the "zone of peace" and the "zone of war."[29] Burnham concisely explained this concept in his 1964 classic, *Suicide of the West:*

> "The zone of peace" means the region that is already subject to communist rule; and the label signifies that within their region the communists will not permit any political tendency, violent or non-violent, whether purely internal or assisted from without, to challenge their rule. "The zone of war" is the region where communist rule is not yet, but in due course will be, established; and within the zone of war the communists promote, assist and where possible lead political tendencies, violent or non-violent, democratic or revolutionary, that operate against non-communist rule.[30]

Thus, according to Burnham, the major threat to the West was not a direct Soviet attack on Western Europe, but the gradual expansion of Soviet power via surrogate forces combined with, and assisted by, the gradual collapse of Western resolve. Burnham thus accurately forecast not only the "Brezhnev Doctrine," which gave explicit expression to the "peace zone/war zone" dichotomy, but also the principal salients of Soviet conflict strategy in the third world that unfolded more fully in the 1970s.

The creation of the North Atlantic Treaty Organization in 1949 marked an historic departure in U.S. foreign policy. Mackinder's theory offered the geopolitical foundations for this departure, but it was Nicholas Spykman who turned this theory into central prescriptions for U.S. policy.

During the war, Spykman had written an elaborate geopolitical critique of American isolationism in *America's Strategy in World Politics* (1942). The book's two central themes were that the United States: (1) must adopt a policy of *Realpolitik* in the recognition that "power" was the real governing force in international relations, and (2) must recognize that the Eurasian power balance directly impacts on American security.

The American scholar most frequently identified as the founder of the "power politics" school of thought is Hans Morganthau. His book, *Politics Among Nations,* written in 1948, became a standard text for the (new) study of international relations in American universities.[31] Yet, six years before the publication of Morganthau's book, Nicholas Spykman had anticipated many of its ideas.

"The struggle for power," wrote Spykman, "is identified with the struggle for survival, and the improvement of the relative power position becomes the primary objective of the internal and external policy of states. All else is secondary, because in the last instance only power can achieve the objectives of foreign policy."[32] Spykman was well aware of the tendency among American policymakers to inject moralism into foreign policy. He counseled,

> The statesman who conducts foreign policy can concern himself with values of justice, fairness, and tolerance only to the extent that they contribute to or do not interfere with the power objective. They can be used instrumentally as moral justification for the power quest, but they must be discarded the moment their application brings weakness. The search for power is not made for the achievement of moral values; moral values are used to facilitate the attainment of power.[33]

Spykman believed that each nation's quest for security inevitably led to conflict, because "the margin of security for one is the margin of danger for the other, and alliance must, therefore, be met by counter-alliance and armament by counter-armament in an eternal competitive struggle for power. Thus it has been in all periods of history."[34]

But it was the second theme of *America's Strategy in World Politics* that earned Spykman a lasting place in the field of geopolitics. This theme was that "the first line of defense of the United States lies in the preservation of a balance of power in Europe and Asia."[35] Spykman explained that throughout the nineteenth century the United States enjoyed the *de facto* protection of the British fleet for its hemispheric security, leaving America free to pursue her "manifest destiny." The tides of the twentieth century had changed all this.

Echoing Mackinder's concept, Spykman posited that "the position of the United States in regard to Europe as a whole is . . . identical to the position of Great Britain in regard to the European Continent.... We have an interest in the European balance as the British have an interest in the continental balance."[36] Writing when the war's outcome was still in doubt, Spykman warned of the consequences of a victory for the Axis powers: "If the German-Japanese Alliance should be victorious on the Eurasian landmass and become free to turn its whole strength against the New World, the United States could not defend the hemisphere."[37]

Thus, the immediate imperative was the defeat of the Axis powers. But this was not enough, according to Spykman, because "the end of a war is not the end of the power struggle."[38] He argued, "Because of the distribution of landmasses and military potentials, a balance of power in the transatlantic and transpacific zones is an absolute prerequisite for the independence of the New World and the preservation of the power position of the United States. There is no safe defensive position on this side of the oceans. Hemisphere defense is no defense at all."[39] Isolationism will not guarantee us peace or security. On the contrary, "it will be cheaper in the long run to remain a working member of the European power zone than to withdraw for short intermissions to our insular domain only to be forced to apply later the whole of our national strength to redress a balance that might have needed but a slight weight at the beginning."[40]

In *The Geography of the Peace,* Spykman's last work (published posthumously in 1944), he expressed relief at the imminent defeat of the Axis powers, but urged American policymakers not to forget the peril which had faced them earlier in the war:

> The most significant fact . . . about the situation which confronted us when, at the beginning of 1942, Germany and Japan had achieved a good part of their objectives was the existence of a political alliance between them. We were then confronted with the possibility of complete encirclement, in which case we might have had to face the unified power of the whole Eurasian landmass. The strength of the power centers of the Eastern Hemisphere would then have been overpowering. It would have been impossible for us to preserve our independence and security. If we are to avoid the conclusion of such an encirclement in the future, our constant concern in peacetime must be to see that no nation or alliance of nations is allowed to emerge as a dominating power in either of the two regions of the Old World from which our security could be threatened.[41]

Hence, he argued, "the safety and independence of this country can be preserved only by a foreign policy that will make it impossible for the Eurasian landmass to harbor overwhelming dominant power in Europe and the Far East."[42]

U.S. policy during the Cold War was based essentially on the three geopolitical factors discussed above: (1) America's security would be gravely imperiled if all or most of Eurasia should become politically dominated by a hostile power (Spykman and Mackinder); (2) the power that controlled the heartland of Eurasia—the Soviet Union—posed the greatest threat of Eurasian domination (Mackinder); and (3) the Soviet Union, guided by its revolutionary ideology, would seek to expand its global power through surrogate forces (Burnham and others).

Viewed in this light, American foreign policy, notwithstanding inevitable discontinuities of policy in a democratic nation, generally (perhaps even "instinctively") was based on those geopolitical precepts. The postwar alliances forged by the United States—most prominently NATO, CENTO, and SEATO—were designed to counter direct Soviet pressures on the rimland of Eurasia, as was the U.S. entente with Communist China. Direct U.S. military interventions in the Korean and Vietnam Wars, as well as in Guatemala, the Dominican Republic and Grenada, were designed to counter the expansion of Soviet power through surrogate forces, as were the U.S. policies of assistance to anti-communist forces in Nicaragua, Angola, and Kampuchea. American support for such countries as Israel, Egypt, Saudi Arabia, Iran (before the fall of the Shah), Pakistan, and Oman was designed to block the expansion of Soviet power into the Middle East/Persian Gulf region. Our specific policies were not always wise or effective, but they did hew to fairly consistent geopolitical considerations.

If the principal bond of American foreign policies since World War II was thus geopolitical, that bond came under increasing challenge. The extent of that challenge was reflected, intellectually, in the virtual eclipse of geopolitics in the American academic realm beginning in the late 1960s. It was reflected, politically, in the deepening cracks in the postwar bipartisan consensus during the decades of the 1970s and 1980s.

The phenomenon's causes were complex. They seemed to center on America's painful experience in Vietnam. Yet, the intellectual challenge to geopolitics antedates Vietnam. It came apace with the advent of nuclear weapons of mass destruction and the long-range means of their delivery—and the notion that this "military revolution" had transfigured the globe, rendering obsolete such "traditional" theories of power as geopolitics.

One of the most cogent discussions of the application of geopolitical thought to the nuclear age was provided by the U.S. strategic analyst, Colin Gray, in his book, *The Geopolitics of the Nuclear Era*[43] In sixty-seven pages, Gray presented a geopolitical framework for understanding Cold War international relations.

Relying heavily on the concepts of Mackinder and Spykman. Gray used classic geopolitical terminology: the Soviet Union was the "Heartland superpower," Western Europe and non-Soviet Asia were the Eurasian "Rimlands," and the United States was the "insular maritime superpower." Moreover, he dispensed with such standard clichés concerning the East-West relationship as "mistrust," "misunderstanding," "managing the relationship," "causing tensions," and so on. The governing force in international relations, according to Gray, was power. The United States and the Soviet Union were engaged in a permanent struggle, the immediate objects of which were the Rimlands of Eurasia. Control of all or most of the Rimlands by the Soviet Union would have given the Kremlin overwhelming political dominance on the Eurasian-African "World Island." Therefore, the overriding geopolitical goal of American foreign policy since 1945 was to prevent that contingency.

Nuclear weapons, Gray explained, must be viewed *within* that geopolitical framework. They are a part of and therefore subordinate to balance-of-power considerations. He warned, "In geopolitical perspective, the American defense community has yet to come to terms with the likely consequences of parity, let alone inferiority. Strategic parity means that the United States has no margin of strategic nuclear strength which could be invoked on behalf of endangered friends and allies in Eurasia"[44]

For forty years the Soviet Union enjoyed a geographical and conventional military power advantage with respect to the Eurasian Rimland. Throughout that period, the United States sought to offset this imbalance with nuclear weapons. In the 1970s, however, in the face of a massive Soviet buildup, U.S. strategic nuclear superiority receded into a position of at best "parity," if not inferiority. That dramatic shift in the nuclear balance affected both Soviet and European attitudes: it emboldened a more aggressive Soviet foreign policy, expressed in the invasion of Afghanistan, and it convinced Europeans of the declining credibility of the American "extended deterrent" over Western Europe—the basis of the U.S. postwar "guaranty" to Europe in the Atlantic Pact.

According to Gray, arms control efforts that sought to confirm nuclear "parity" ignored fundamental geopolitical realities. In the long run, "parity" could not adequately counter the enormous conventional military advantage of the Soviets and their permanent geographical advantages. That left the Western Alliance with two options, according to Gray: "either the maritime alliance [NATO] must sustain a very robust local denial capability, or the United States must invest in a significant margin of strategic nuclear superiority."[45] The first option was politically infeasible; the second option was an arms control heresy. Yet, what answer was there to Gray's ominous questions:

> How are the Eurasian-African Rimlands to be defended against the Heartland power, if strategic parity (or, more likely, parity-plus) is conceded to that power? If superiority in the European theater is conceded? And if anyone, worldwide, who can read a newspaper or listen to a radio can learn that the Soviet Union is on the ascendant in gaining influence in potential (and actual) base areas in Africa and South Asia?[46]

Gray also rejected the "neo-Mahanian" view in the United States that naval superiority could substitute for inadequate ground forces in Europe. "The Soviet Navy," he wrote, "may, and should, be blown out of the water, its forward facilities on African and South Asian littorals also demolished; but time would not be on the side of the maritime alliance. By compelling the maritime alliance to fight hard for unhindered access to Eurasia, the Soviet Navy would be buying time for Soviet conquest of critical portions of the Rimlands (should Blitzkrieg campaign overrun its time-table). In the world of the 1980's and 1990's, an eventual *total* naval victory for the United States would be of little value if, in the meantime, the peninsular European bridgehead were lost."[47]

The combination of geographical position, conventional military superiority and a standoff at the strategic-nuclear level gave the Soviet Union an overall military and, therefore, political advantage over the United States in the struggle for Europe. That implication did not escape the notice of statesmen and strategists on both sides of the Atlantic. In 1982, Franz Josef Strauss, former defense minister of the Federal Republic of Germany, warned, "The principal danger to the West...is not a war in the sense of a large-scale military conflict, but rather the Soviet Union's harnessing of its mounting military capabilities to a process of political intimidation, with the long-term

objective of achieving first the neutralization of Western Europe and
then the Sovietization of all Europe."[48] A year later, General Bernard
Rogers, Supreme Allied Commander in Europe, asked, "How long
can we permit the gap between NATO and Warsaw Pact force capabilities to widen before the military situation is so adverse that NATO
nations find themselves politically intimidated, economically coerced
and subject to blackmail?"[49]

As was noted above, Colin Gray proposed two basic alternatives
for escape from NATO's Cold War predicament: (1) establishing a
"robust local denial capability," or (2) re-attaining clear-cut nuclear
superiority. As a matter of policy, Gray's two alternatives were com-
promised into a single prescription: (1) an improved NATO conventional denial capability in Europe, and (2) a more credible U.S.
nuclear strategy and force structure.[50]

The first element of the prescription required a concerted harnessing of technological advances in the West relevant to conventional defenses: particularly precision-guided munitions and "deep-
strike" capabilities designed to disrupt and deny any potential Warsaw Pact conventional attack. This included the wherewithal for an
"extended air-defense" (that is antimissile defense) proposed by West
German Defense Minister Manfred Woerner.[51] The second element
in the prescription entailed the urgent modernization of the U.S. strategic arsenal in survivable, counter-force capabilities (e.g., MX and
Minuteman missiles) which reinvigorated the U.S. "nuclear guaranty" to the Alliance.

More important than any specific measures adopted, however,
was the recognition that the size and structure of Western forces,
and the strategies for their use, should be determined by geopolitical
realities, rather than by abstract principles of "balance," particularly
in the arms control context. Weapons "freezes," "equal" reductions,
"zero solutions," and other ostensibly equitable or balanced proposals ignored the geopolitical advantages enjoyed by the Soviet Union
by virtue of its control of Eastern Europe and the Heartland. Arms
control, like all other facets of our foreign and defense policies, should
be viewed and pursued within a global geopolitical context.[52]

The Soviet view of the world was based on what they termed the
"correlation of forces." This was a comprehensive measurement of
power that included such objective factors as military forces and
economic, social, political and geographical considerations, as well
as subjective factors such as a given nation's—or alliance's—unity,

"morale," intentions, and resolve. The "correlation of forces" thus served as an explicit guide to Soviet global strategy, which was geared—just as explicitly—to changing the "correlation" in the Soviets' favor.

The "correlation of forces" was essentially a geopolitical concept. We may recall that Mackinder, too, introduced into his theory such subjective elements as the "virility" and "organization" of competing peoples. The Soviet concept was comprehensively global and cast in a "zero-sum" mold, holding that the loss of American or Western influence and power in a given locality or region reduced the relative global power position of the "imperialist bloc," thereby commensurately enhancing the relative power position of the Soviet Union and the "fraternal socialist states." This was so even when lost Western influence in a particular locality or region was not directly supplanted by Soviet power and influence—Iran being a perfect example. Those who chided the Reagan administration for viewing developments in Central America, for example, in an "East-West" rather than a "regional" context should be aware of the fact that that was precisely how those developments were viewed from Moscow.

Geopolitical concepts do not provide statesmen with specific policy prescriptions, setting forth when it is appropriate to use such tools as military force, economic and military assistance, or covert operations, let alone determining the means and content of diplomacy with allies and adversaries. Rather, geopolitical concepts offer a global framework within which both grand strategy and specific policies can be formulated and implemented.

Unfortunately, as Halford Mackinder so keenly recognized over sixty years ago, democracies often succumb to the temptation of basing their foreign policy on ideals rather than geopolitical realities. Woodrow Wilson succumbed to this temptation at the end of World War I, as did Franklin Roosevelt near the end of World War II. Both leaders placed their sincere hope for peace in a world organization that would represent "mankind."

Similarly during the Cold War, American idealists placed their hopes for peace and a better world in disarmament treaties and "democratic" revolutions. Such idealism may be an expression of American societal values, but it can be projected outward onto a values-diverse world only at the risk of exposing the wellspring of those values— our society itself—to enormous dangers. We have witnessed the consequences for U.S. policy when the "corrupt Thieu regime" in Saigon came to overshadow the implications of a communist take-over of Indochina, and when the "crimes of the Shah" obscured the imperative of Western access to the Persian Gulf. And we confronted the danger in the 1980s of permitting alleged "human rights violations" by the Contras in Nicaragua to distort our view of U.S. strategic stakes in Central America that was under attack by surrogate forces of the Soviet Union.

Such idealism was not limited to the liberal sectors of the American political spectrum. Some U.S. conservatives were reluctant to recognize the "opening" to Communist China staged by President Richard Nixon during his first term. The Sino-Soviet rift—between the two most powerful communist nations and, more important, the two largest countries on the Eurasian landmass—was one of the crucial geopolitical developments of the second half of the twentieth century. Pleas on behalf of the position and claims of the Republic of China (Taiwan), however morally valid, did not alter the global geopolitical realities. An independent and antagonistic China compelled the Soviet Union to sustain significant military forces on its long border with the PRC forces that could otherwise have been added to the already prohibitive weight of the Soviet military posture in Europe.

Other conservatives voiced doubts about the wisdom of maintaining a large U.S. ground presence in Europe. They correctly argued that our European allies were quite capable of doing more in their own conventional defense, permitting the United States to concentrate on its capabilities to meet contingencies in other important areas of the world, such as the Persian Gulf region, and to buttress its strategic deterrent. That would have made for a more logical division of resources among Alliance members. But the logical is not always the politically feasible. Perhaps the decision to substantially reduce American forces on the continent would, as commentators like Irving Kristol and Senator Sam Nunn suggested, have "shocked" the Europeans into spending more for their security. Yet, could we have afforded to take such a risk? Were we prepared to live with the consequences if Europeans were, instead, "shocked" into political accommodation with the Soviet Union?

In geopolitical terms, China and Western Europe during the Cold War were two large weights on the peripheries of the Eurasian landmass adjacent to the Soviet Heartland. The effective control of either territory by the Soviet Union—through direct conquest or political hegemony—would have drastically shifted the "correlation of world forces" in Moscow's favor. Mackinder's ominous vision of a Heartland-based world empire would have come precariously close to realization.

Thus, in geopolitical terms, the alignments of Western Europe and China during the Cold War could not be viewed separately. Both eventually were crucial players in denying the Soviets hegemony over Eurasia and overwhelming political predominance on the World Island. The loss or neutralization of either power center would have set in motion an inexorable series of global power trends leading to a relentless retreat by the United States into a "Fortress America," increasingly isolated economically, politically, and spiritually from the world-at-large, and with the psychological incubus of beleaguerment bearing down on its free institutions and values.

That prospect was averted because the United States dealt with the world as it was, not as we wished it to be. We formulated a grand strategy based on fundamental geopolitical realities. Containment of Soviet Heartland power was the cornerstone of that strategy -- meaning our ability to project adequate power along the periphery of the Soviet empire in an arc extending from Norway, across Central Europe, through the Balkans, the Middle East, and Southwest Asia, curving from South-Central Asia to Korea and Japan. That translated into maintaining and strengthening NATO, helping to stabilize the Middle East-Persian Gulf region, strengthening our relationship with China, and maintaining the U.S. forward positions in Australia, the Philippines, Korea, and Japan. But to direct containment of Soviet power was added an effective strategy for countering indirect Soviet thrusts spearheaded by surrogate forces in Africa, Asia, and our own hemisphere. The first step in developing such a strategy was a clearer understanding of the geopolitical implications of ostensibly "local" or "regional" conflicts.

Most Americans might be startled to discover that American foreign policy during the Cold War had its intellectual roots in concepts first formulated over eighty years ago by a British geographer. Events since then fully justify Colin Gray's assessment of Mackinder as "the most influential and perceptive geopolitical thinker." As Robert Nisbet has commented, "Every geopolitical apprehension that Sir Halford Mackinder expressed some six decades ago in his *Democratic Ideals and Reality* has been fulfilled."[53]

Mackinder, and later thinkers such as Spykman and Burnham, were able to look beneath and beyond the immediate political events, grasping the essential and enduring aspects of international relations. They recognized and emphasized the two most permanent and there- fore most significant factors in world affairs: geography and power. They observed and analyzed events with cold objectivity, but did so in order to help preserve and protect the small portion of the world where liberty and freedom exist. It is up to a new generation to en- sure that their counsels were not in vain.

Notes

1.   George F. Kennan, *American Diplomacy* (Chicago: University of Chicago Press, 1951), P. 99.
2.   Halford J. Mackinder, *Democratic Ideals and Reality* (New York: W.W. Norton & Co., 1962), p. 250. This 1962 edition contains the original 1919 work, as well as "The Geographical Pivot of History" and "The Round World and the Winning of the Peace." All references to Mackinder's writings are from the 1962 edition.
3.   Ibid., p. 254.
4.   Ibid., p. 262.
5.   Ibid.
6.   Ibid., p. 263.
7.   Ibid., p. 2.
8.   Ibid., pp. 73-74.
9.   Ibid., p. 53.
10.   Ibid., p. 65.
11.   Ibid., p. 70.
12.   Ibid., p. 125.
13.   Ibid., p. 139.
14.   Ibid., p. 149.
15.   Ibid., p. 150.
16.   Ibid., p. 114.
17.   Ibid., p. 276.
18.   Ibid., pp. 272-273.
19.   Ibid., p. 277.
20.   Raymond Aron, *The Century of Total War* (Boston: The Beacon Press, 1955), p. 111.
21.   Nicholas Spykman, *The Geography of the Peace* (New York: Harcourt, Brace & Co., 1944), p. 43.
22.   James Burnham, *The Struggle for the World* (New York: John Day Co., 1947).
23.   James Burnham, *Containment or Liberation?*(New York: John Day Co., 1953), p
24.   Burnham, *The Struggle for the World,* p. 96
25.   James Burnham, *The Coming Defeat of Communism* (New York: John Day Co., 1950), p. 14.
26.   Burnham, *Containment or Liberation?* pp. 113—114.
27.   Ibid., p. 114.
28.   Burnham, *The Coming Defeat of Communism,* p. 83.
29.   These terms were first used by Robert Strausz-Hupé, James Dougherty, William Kintner, and Alvin Cottrell in their 1959 work, *Protracted Conflict,* but the concept was implicit in Burnham's earlier works.

30. James Burnham, *Suicide of the West* (Chicago: Regnery Books, 1985), pp. 227—228.
31. Hans J. Morganthau, *Politics Among Nations* (New York: Alfred A. Knopf, 1949). Morganthau first discussed this topic in *Scientific Man vs. Power Politics* (1946).
32. Nicholas Spykman, *America's Strategy in World Politics* (New York: Harcourt, Brace & Co., 1942), p. 18.
33. Ibid., p. 18.
34. Ibid., p. 24.
35. Ibid., p. 4.
36. Ibid., p. 124.
37. Ibid., p. 444.
38. Ibid., p. 457.
39. Ibid.
40. Ibid., pp. 467—468.
41. Spykman, *The Geography of the Peace,* (New York: Harcourt, Brace & Co., 1944), p. 34.
42. Ibid., p. 60.
43. Colin Gray, *The Geopolitics of the Nuclear Era: Heartland, Rimlands, and the Technological Revolution* (New York: Crane, Russak & Co., Inc., 1977).
44. Ibid., p. 62.
45. Ibid., p. 53.
46. Ibid.
47. Ibid., p. 59.
48. Franz Josef Strauss, "Manifesto of a German Atlanticist," *Strategic Review,* Summer 1982, p. 13.
49. Bernard Rogers, "Greater Flexibility for NATO's Flexible Response," *Strategic Review,* Spring 1983, p. 14.
50. In Gray's most recent writing on this topic, he does not specifically advocate nuclear superiority. He advises NATO to focus on "denying the prompt acquisition of important territorial 'prizes'; supporting, threatening, reviving, or creating continental distractions; gaining leverage through seizure of important assets; shifting the balance of forces progressively in one's favor; flexibility and surprise in application of force from the sea; and eroding the enemy's confidence in the likelihood of victory." See "Keeping the Soviets Landlocked," *National Interest,* Summer 1986, pp. 35-36.
51. Manfred Woerner, "A Missile Defense for NATO Europe," *Strategic Review,* Winter 1986, p. 19.
52. This is especially true of the ongoing Mutual andBalanced Force Reductions in Europe (MBFR) negotiations. As Carnes Lord recently explained:".., any mutual withdrawal of U.S. and Soviet forces from Europe would have grossly asymmetrical consequences. Any U.S. units removed from Central Europe would have to be withdrawn thousands of miles across the Atlantic to the United States, while Soviet troops withdrawn to their homeland could remain less than 500 miles from the inner-German border. This asymmetry has grown increasingly severe during the lifetime of MBFR, as steady improvements in the quality and quantity of Soviet forces in Europe have increased Soviet chances of a quick victory and made more problematic the resupply and reinforcement of NATO's central front by the United States." Carnes Lord, "The MFBR Mystery," *American Spectator,* June 1986, p. 14.
53. Robert Nisbet, *History of the Idea of Progress* (New York: Basic Books, Inc., 1980), p. 331.

6

The Geopolitics of the Post-Cold War World

Ever since the dramatic, revolutionary upheavals began in Central and Eastern Europe and, within the Soviet Union in 1989, the American foreign policy establishment has been searching for a new "Mr. X"—a new foreign policy guru who, emulating the original Mr. X, George F. Kennan, will set down on paper the broad outlines of a national security doctrine designed to guide American statesmen in the next decade and beyond. Kennan is credited with being the theoretical "father" of the "containment" doctrine which, arguably, served as a broad policy guide to every presidential administration from Truman through Reagan. Kennan's "long telegram" from Moscow in 1946 and his seminal article in *Foreign Affairs* the following year, examined the nature of the Soviet military and political threat to the West and advocated a policy of "long term, patient but firm and vigilant containment" of Soviet/Russian expansionist tendencies.[1]

As implemented by successive U.S. presidential administrations, containment meant the formation of political and military alliances, the deployment of U.S. air, land, and naval forces at key points around the globe, the buildup of conventional and nuclear armed forces, and, on occasion, war. Although Kennan subsequently distanced himself from the military aspects of the containment doctrine (in part, it appears, due to his fear of a nuclear war between the superpowers),[2] the gradual collapse of the Soviet empire confirmed his original belief that containment would "promote tendencies which must eventually find their outlet in either the break-up or the gradual mellowing of Soviet power."[3]

Soviet power first mellowed then collapsed. Initially, the external Soviet empire in Eastern and Central Europe dissolved. The internal Soviet empire was then transformed as a result of political, ethnic, and national conflicts, and economic distress. All fifteen Soviet republics eventually became independent. The unsuccessful coup attempt in August 1991 by communist hard-liners accelerated that revolutionary process. The Communist Party was formally suspended throughout the country and the Russian republic, under the leadership of Boris Yeltsin, emerged as the dominant political force in the former Soviet Union. The Baltic republics were the first to declare their independence and receive diplomatic recognition from many Western nations. Eleven of the remaining twelve republics initially formed a Commonwealth of Independent States headquartered in Minsk and attempted to adopt a common military policy.

Meanwhile, Germany is again one nation, an economic powerhouse in the heart of the European peninsula; the European Community strives toward a United States of Europe; Japan continues to thrive economically and hints at playing a more prominent global role; China attempts to mix political repression with economic decentralization; and several so-called "Third World" countries continue to acquire "First World" military arsenals, including weapons of mass destruction.

Russia's military, of course, remains formidable. It can still field a potentially powerful land army. It still possesses thousands of nuclear warheads and delivery systems. Moreover, Russia continues to have interests that diverge from our own in some parts of the world. The ideological aspect of the Cold War may in fact have been terminated, but the geopolitical aspect remains.

Those who would assume the mantle of the new Mr. X have been busy writing op-ed pieces and articles proposing new grand strategies to deal with the "new" post-Cold War world.[4] The search for a new Mr. X, unquestionably, has fostered an important debate on the future national security strategy of the United States. Unfortunately, that debate has for the most part overlooked the fact that George Kennan's containment proposal was based not on the temporary circumstances of the post-World War II order, but on geopolitical realities which have been recognized since the founding of our country.

Kennan's advocacy of containment stemmed from the recognition that America's security was greatly affected by the balance of power on the Eurasian landmass. Kennan was among the first Americans to realize that World War II resulted in a grave imbalance in favor of the Soviet Union on the Eurasian continent which could only be rectified by a strong U.S. commitment to the devastated nations within easy reach of Soviet power. The stationing in peace-time of large numbers of American troops in Europe and Asia was, indeed, a great departure for U.S. foreign policy. But this develop-ment and the whole containment policy resulted from the imbalance created by the war, not from a sudden realization that the Eurasian balance of power affected America's security interests.

As mentioned above, since the founding of our country, states-men and strategists have noted the relationship between America's security and the Eurasian balance of power. Alexander Hamilton believed that Americans owed their independence and security, in part, to the rivalry among Europe's great powers. It is "impossible," he wrote, that any of the major European powers "should consent that the other should become master of this country."[6] Unwilling to base our security solely on that rivalry, Hamilton urged the creation of a strong navy in order to erect a security system "superior to the control of all transatlantic force or influence, and able to dictate the terms of the connection between the old and the new world."[7]

Another of the Founding Fathers, John Adams, in his autobiogra-phy, reflected on the importance of the Anglo-French rivalry to the cause of American independence. America obtained her temporary alliance with France against Great Britain, Adams explained, because France "could not endure Britain's height of power and preeminence." France's "rank, her consideration in Europe, and even her safety and independence were at stake" in Britain's war with the American colonies, according to Adams.[8]

Of course, if the rivalry among the European great powers ceased to exist either because of alliances or conquests, America's security could be threatened from the Old World. This geopolitical appre-hension was expressed by two prominent American statesmen dur-ing and after the period of Napoleon's domination of Europe. Con-gressman John Randolph, speaking shortly before the War of 1812 when Napoleon had conquered all of Europe except Portugal and the Balkan peninsula and had forced Russia, Prussia, and Austria into an alliance with France, courageously warned his colleagues who advocated war with Britain that it would be folly for the United States to fight the British, since Britain was the only power that held France in check. Randolph suggested that the United States would be gravely imperiled if France defeated Britain and gained access to the British navy. "Suppose France in possession of British naval power," he asked rhetorically, "what would be your condition?" "What," he asked further, "could you expect if they [the French] were the uncontrolled lords of the ocean?"[9]

A few years later, after Napoleon's invasion of Russia, Thomas Jefferson opined that is was not in the United States' interest "that all Europe should be reduced to a single monarchy....Surely none of us wish to see Bonaparte conquer Russia and lay thus at his feet the whole continent of Europe. This done, England would be but a breakfast....Put all Europe into his [Napoleon's] hands, and he might spare such a force to be sent in British ships as I would as leave not have to encounter."[10] Writing subsequent to Napoleon's defeat in Russia, Jefferson noted that had France triumphed in Russia, Napoleon would have become "sole lord of the continent of Europe" which would have led to the "establishment...of another Roman empire, spreading vassalage and depravity over the face of the globe." He expressed the hope that "all nations may recover [from the Napoleonic Wars] and retain their independence; [and] that a salutary balance may be ever maintained among nations."[11]

Randolph and Jefferson clearly perceived that America's security could be endangered by a European conqueror who availed himself of the immense resources of the Old World. They surely would have agreed with Thomas Boylston Adams, who, with remarkable foresight, stated in October 1799 that "it must always happen, so long as America is an independent Republic or nation, that the balance of power in Europe will continue to be of utmost importance to her welfare."[12]

Fear of European intervention and encroachments in the Americas led to the formulation of the Monroe Doctrine in 1823. President James Monroe announced that the United States would consider any attempt by the European Powers "to extend their system to any portion of this hemisphere as dangerous to our peace and safety."[13] Two decades later, President Polk reaffirmed this doctrine by telling the Congress that the United States "can not in silence permit any European interference on the North American continent and will be ready to resist [such interference] at any and all hazards."[14] A year after Polk's statement, Senate Foreign Relations Committee Chairman William Allen declared that "any effort of the powers of Europe to...extend the European system of government upon this continent...would be...dangerous to the liberties of the people of

America, and therefore will incur...the prompt resistance of the United States."[15] In 1895, Secretary of State Richard Olney restated the enduring purpose of the Monroe Doctrine: "It is that no European power or combination of European powers shall forcibly deprive an American state of the right and power of self-government and of shaping for itself its own political fortunes and destinies."[16]

The United States during the nineteenth century, of course, had not yet acquired the power to enforce the Monroe Doctrine. Our hemispheric security, as Norman Graebner pointed out, was maintained by a number of factors including the Atlantic Ocean, the British Navy, and the Eurasian balance of power.[17] Implicit in the Monroe Doctrine was the recognition that America's security and independence could be threatened by a power or alliance of powers in Europe, and that the United States should adopt policies designed to counter any such threat.

It was during the latter part of the nineteenth century and early twentieth century that geopolitical theorists began to focus on the global distribution of political power and its effects on specific regions and individual nations. This was no mere coincidence because, as Sir Halford Mackinder insightfully pointed out in 1904, the world had recently completed the "Columbian epoch" during which "the outline of the map of the world [had] been completed with approximate accuracy." For four hundred years, explorers in search of new worlds traversed the globe's deserts, plains, mountains, valleys, rivers and seas, and consequently revealed the essential geographical features of the earth; and as Mackinder noted, "the missionary, the conqueror, the farmer, the miner, and. . . the engineer... followed so closely in the traveler's footsteps that the world, in its remote borders, has hardly been revealed before we must chronicle its virtually complete political appropriation." The world, according to Mackinder, was now a "closed political system" where "every explosion of social forces, instead of being dissipated in a surrounding circuit of unknown space and barbaric chaos, will be sharply re-echoed from the far side of the globe, and weak elements in the political and economic organism of the world will be shattered in consequence."[18]

Beginning in 1904 and continuing over the course of four decades, Mackinder sketched and re-sketched a geopolitical map of the world which included three essential elements: one great continent composed of Europe, Asia, and Africa (the "World-Island"), many smaller islands such as Britain, Japan, Australia, and the Americas, and one great ocean covering three-fourths of the globe. He identified the northern-central core of Eurasia as the "pivot region" or Heartland from which a sufficiently organized and armed power or alliance of powers could threaten the rest of the world. Geography and rapid means of land transportation presented the Heartland power with the opportunity to expand into the remaining parts of the World-Island without taking to the ocean. Moreover, the Heartland citadel was itself inaccessible to sea power since its major rivers emptied into either the frozen Arctic Ocean or inland seas. Mackinder warned the maritime powers of Britain and the United States that a Heartland-based power which acquired control over the resources and manpower of the World-Island could construct the world's most powerful navy and thereby defeat the maritime powers in their own element.[19]

In 1943, Mackinder added an important feature to his geopolitical sketch of the globe that, he indicated, could counterbalance the Heartland power. He called this feature the "Midland Ocean," and described it as encompassing the West European peninsula, Britain, the Atlantic Ocean and the eastern portion of North America.[20] Mackinder's Midland Ocean concept became a political reality with the formation of the North Atlantic Treaty Organization (NATO) in 1949.

Mackinder's detailed and comprehensive geopolitical theories essentially repeated to Americans the warnings uttered previously, if less grandiosely, by their own statesmen: the United States could not remain indifferent to the balance of power on the Eurasian landmass. In fact, his Heartland concept was anticipated in some respects by the American naval historian and strategist, Alfred Thayer Mahan.[21] Mahan, like Mackinder, conceded Eurasian predominance to the geographical area occupied by Russia. Mahan, like Mackinder, urged the sea powers of the world to combine to counterbalance the land power of Russia (and later, Germany). Where the two strategists differed was in their estimation of the relative strengths of the land powers and sea powers, with Mahan favoring the latter and Mackinder favoring the former. Both strategists realized, however, that no single maritime power could effectively counterbalance land power based in the core of Eurasia, and that all the maritime powers would be endangered if the great land powers (Germany or Russia) acquired ready access to the ocean and built powerful navies.

As the First World War approached, the American diplomat, Lewis Einstein, penned a brilliant geopolitical analysis of the security threat to the United States in a British journal, the *National Review*. Reviewing the European power struggles since the founding of our nation, Einstein concluded that the "European balance of power has been such a permanent factor since the birth of the republic that Americans have never realized how its absence would have affected their political status." He noted that Great Britain's resistance to Napoleon in the early 1800s and her navy's *de facto* role in enforcing the Monroe Doctrine thereafter, kept potential European aggressors from our shores. Echoing Mahan and Mackinder (and Jefferson and Randolph), Einstein opined that the "undisputed paramountcy of any nation, both by land and sea, must inevitably make that power a menace and a peril to every other country," and he warned specifically that the United States would suffer a great defeat if the disintegration of the British Empire led to the "erection of a power [Germany] supreme on land and sea."[22]

A similar geopolitical warning to the American people was issued by President Franklin D. Roosevelt during a radio address one year before America's entry into the Second World War. With Germany on the march in Europe and Japan subjugating parts of Asia, FDR explained that "it is a matter of most vital concern to us that European and Asiatic war-makers should not gain control of the oceans which lead to this hemisphere." He expressed a concern about the threat posed to the Western Hemisphere by the united power and resources of the Old World:

> If Great Britain goes down, the Axis powers will control the continents of Europe, Asia, Africa, Australia, and the high seas—and they will be in a position to bring enormous military and naval resources against this hemisphere. It is no exaggeration to say that all of us in the Americas would be living at the point of a gun—a gun loaded with explosive bullets, economic as well as military.[23]

FDR's remarks were reminiscent of Mackinder's warning in 1919 that rule of the World-Island (Europe, Asia, and Africa) by a single power or alliance of powers meant command of the world.[24]

During the Second World War, two American writers elaborated on the geopolitical threat posed by the Old World to the New World. Nicholas Spykman, professor of history at Yale University, and the popular polemicist Walter Lippmann recognized, in Lippmann's words, that "the facts of geography are permanent."[25] Reviewing those facts, Spykman posited that the United States and Britain were islands offshore of the Eurasian landmass. Like Mackinder, Spykman recognized Russia's predominant position in the interior of Eurasia; but like Mahan, he believed the sea powers of Britain and the U.S. could maintain access to the Eurasian "rimland" and thereby control "the destinies of the world."[26] World politics, according to Spykman, was a continuing contest between land powers and sea powers for control of the Eurasian rimland. It was imperative, Spykman believed, for the United States to focus its foreign policy efforts toward preventing a power or alliance of powers from organizing and uniting the resources of the Old World. America could only do this, reasoned Spykman, by remaining a "working member of the European power zone," because "the first line of defense of the United States lies in the preservation of a balance of power in Europe and Asia."[27]

Lippmann similarly argued that the United States "cannot afford to be isolated against the combined forces of the Old World."[28] Invoking Jefferson, Madison, and Monroe, Lippmann claimed that "the strategic defenses of the United States . . . extend across both oceans and to all transoceanic lands from which an attack by sea or by air can be launched."[29] "American security," argued Lippmann, "has always. . . extended to the coastline of Europe, Africa and Asia."[30]

Both Spykman and Lippmann believed that their geopolitical concepts applied in times of peace as well as during wartime, and both expressed the apprehension that following the Second World War, Soviet Russia could pose the same threat to American security that Hitlerian and Wilhelmine Germany had posed. Their literary efforts were undertaken to prevent a third global conflict by calling America's attention to its permanent security interests on the Eurasian landmass.

As the above discussion demonstrates, the original Mr. X, George Kennan, was not writing in an intellectual vacuum when he sent the "long telegram" in 1946 and penned his famous article in *Foreign Affairs* in 1947. This fact does not detract from the perceptiveness and persuasiveness of Kennan's containment proposal; it merely places it in historical perspective. The theoretical basis of containment—that America's security could be threatened by a dominant Eurasian land power—was not a novel idea in American foreign policy. (What was a radical departure from previous policies was the decision to station large numbers of U.S. ground troops on the Eurasian continent during peacetime.) Colin S. Gray, contemporary

America's foremost scholar of geopolitical thought, noted that although "George Kennan may not acknowledge the debt,... the 'Long Telegram' from Moscow. . . and the article by 'X' in *Foreign Affairs* . . . directly or indirectly bear the hallmark of Mackinder's worldview."[31] And, one might add, of Jefferson's, Randolph's, Mahan's, Einstein's and Spykman's worldviews.

Kennan's containment proposal was an application of timeless geopolitical concepts to the particular circumstances of the post-World War II world. Those same geopolitical concepts are equally applicable to the particular circumstances of the post-Cold War world. Before applying those concepts, let us first summarize the immediate circumstances of the post-Cold War world.

The Soviet Union's empire in Eastern and Central Europe has collapsed. Freely elected, non-communist governments in several Eastern and Central European states are not beholden to Moscow, and the Russian Army has wholly withdrawn from those states. East Germany is now part of a united Germany.

The Soviet empire has been replaced by Russia. Throughout Russia and the former Soviet Union, food "shortages" caused by inefficient transportation systems, bureaucratic red tape and individual hoarding have created region-wide turmoil. The bungled coup attempt in August 1991 sapped whatever legitimacy remained from the Communist Party of the Soviet Union (CPSU). Gorbachev, though widely praised in the West, had lost favor with the Soviet populace, even before the coup attempt. Gorbachev resigned as general secretary of the CPSU, allied himself, at least temporarily, with Yeltsin, and formed an ineffectual central governing body which consisted of himself and the presidents of most of the other republics. That governing body subsequently gave way to the new Commonwealth of Independent States.

The Russian empire has thus contracted and mellowed during this "time of troubles." Russia's military, however, still fields a powerful land army, a blue-ocean navy, a multi-tentacled intelligence and espionage apparatus, and thousands of nuclear weapons and delivery systems. The future is highly uncertain, but this much remains clear: the Heartland will continue to be occupied by a great power which possesses a large military establishment, tremendous amounts of natural resources, nuclear weapons and a history of imperial expansion. Most of the Heartland is controlled by the Great Russian Republic which extends over 6.5 million square miles, has a population estimated at 146 million, and contains large quantities of natural resources. The Russian Republic could unquestionably field a modern, powerful military, and, due to its geographical location, could expand in all directions save the north. It is situated astride much smaller and less populated republics, and may be tempted by the wheat fields of Ukraine, the mineral deposits of Kazakhstan, and the lure of the oceans. In fact, shortly after the coup attempt failed in August 1991, Russian President Yeltsin indicated a desire to expand the borders of Russia in the event that Belorussia and the Ukraine attained independent status. Yeltsin and his successors also have demonstrated an unwillingness to tolerate nationalist stirrings among ethnic minorities within the Russian Republic.

The European peninsula is also in a state of flux. Economic unity is on the horizon, but political unity is a distant prospect at best. Furthermore, as the eastern threat decreases, the most persuasive incentive for political unification dissipates. The new principal factor in Europe is the old principal factor: Germany. A united Germany occupies almost 140,000 square miles of territory, holds a population of approximately 78 million people, is an economic powerhouse with even greater potential, and is located in the strategic center of Europe with limited access to the ocean. The larger part of Germany has been a prosperous, democratic nation for forty years. But the smaller, eastern part has been ruled by totalitarian regimes since the early 1930s. This united German nation, a potential economic giant in the center of Europe, faces a reduced Russian threat and a growing power vacuum in Eastern Europe.

The collapse of the Soviet empire increases the relative power position of the People's Republic of China (PRC) in world affairs, but also reduces the incentive for its continuing cooperation with the Western powers. Since the early 1970s, if not before, the PRC acted as a *de facto* American strategic ally in the effort to contain the Soviet Union. The end of the Soviet threat combined with Western antagonism resulting from the crackdown in Tiananmen Square, poses a dilemma for China's communist leaders: where should they apply China's weight on the global scales of power? The communist leaders need Western technology and know-how to modernize their economy, but they may also need to repress democratic forces in China to maintain total power. Political repression, however, antagonizes the sources of the needed technology and stifles the creative entrepreneurial talent required to sustain long-term economic growth.

Whatever China ultimately decides, her immense population, large military, and stockpile of nuclear weapons make her a formidable, if second-rate, world power.

China's geographic location in East Asia gives her access to the ocean and the thriving markets of the Pacific Rim. Her weight in the future global balance of power will depend on how swiftly and effectively she can modernize her economy, increase her trade with the growing Asian economies of Taiwan, South Korea, and Japan, and modernize her armed forces. The United States cannot ignore and should attempt to influence where and how China flexes its geopolitical muscle.

The other Asian world power is Japan. Like Germany in Europe, Japan is the economic powerhouse of Asia. Its economic power, well-educated population (in excess of 120 million), and insular location off-shore the East Asian mainland present Japan with the opportunity to become a great maritime power. Thus far, Japan's leaders have decided against that option, preferring instead to focus the nation's energies toward economic productivity and growth, while relying on the U.S. military for their security needs. With a declining Russian threat and an increasing U.S. trade deficit vis-à-vis Japan, however, America's willingness to continue to provide for Japan's security cannot be taken for granted.

The United States is today the world's only economic and military superpower. Its security commitments remain vast, with military outposts in Europe, Asia, Central America, the Caribbean and Mediterranean seas, the Persian Gulf, and Indian, Pacific, and Atlantic oceans. But as the ideological competition with Moscow has waned, neo-isolationist views have become more respectable, even among hawkish conservatives like Patrick J. Buchanan. The neo-isolationists argue that the declining Russian threat and the rising economic power of Germany and Japan should result in a more equitable sharing of the democracies' defense burden and a reduced U.S. involvement overseas. Having led the Free World to victory in the Cold War, America, according to the neo-isolationists, should attend to its own troubled house—drugs, crime, illiteracy, poor education, and so on.

Other Americans, Wilsonian interventionists, believe that the end of the Cold War is the latest victory in a crusade for democracy throughout the world. In their view, the United States should actively promote democratic causes and groups in foreign lands. The

Wilsonian interventionists cite democratic developments in South Korea, the Philippines, Panama, and South Africa as evidence of the effectiveness of U.S. efforts to promote democracy.

The combined impact of large budget deficits, a worsening domestic economy, and a reduced Russian threat resulted in plans to halve our forces in Europe, lessen our military presence in Asia, and reduce the number of ships in our navy. The euphoria of our ideological victory in the Cold War is clouding our leaders' geopolitical judgment. It is strategic folly, simultaneously, to dramatically reduce our land presence on Eurasia and diminish our ability to transport military manpower and equipment to the continent.

One other aspect of contemporary world affairs that deserves mention is the large size of "Third World" military arsenals. The United States, Soviet Union, China, France, Brazil, and Britain have all contributed to the proliferation of sophisticated weapons and technology throughout the Third World. As a result, countries such as India, Egypt, Israel, and Syria have military arsenals that rival or exceed those of France and Britain in numbers of main battle tanks, armored personnel carriers and combat aircraft. (This was also true of Iraq prior to its defeat by the U.S. and its allies in the Persian Gulf War). Active chemical weapons programs exist in Iraq, Vietnam, Taiwan, North Korea, Syria, Iran, Egypt, Libya, and Israel, while India, Iran, Israel, Egypt, Yemen, Iraq, Kuwait, Saudi Arabia, Syria, North Korea, South Korea, Brazil, Taiwan, Libya, Argentina, and Algeria have surface-to-surface ballistic missiles.[32] In addition, Israel, India, South Africa, Pakistan, North Korea, and Iraq are said to have nuclear weapons or active nuclear weapons programs. (United Nations inspectors discovered, in the wake of the Persian Gulf War, that Iraq's nuclear and chemical weapons programs were far more extensive than originally believed). The combination of Third World arms proliferation and regional antagonisms in the Middle East, Persian Gulf, Southeast Asia, Southwest Asia and other parts of the globe raise the specter of, in Mark Katz's words, "regional hegemons" that could threaten important, even vital, Western interests.[33]

In geopolitical terms, the circumstances of the post-Cold War world reveal a less unevenly balanced Eurasian landmass. Russia continues to occupy the most strategically advantageous region on the globe, the Heartland of Eurasia, but its regime, beset by internal strife, has turned inward. The collapse of the East European empire has created a power vacuum between the Russian and the re-unified

German nation. The European peninsula, however, remains politically divided and militarily unable (or unwilling) to effectively counterbalance the reduced Russian military threat. The coastlands of Asia, in addition to being politically divided, consist of countries that are hostile or antagonistic toward one another (for example, Pakistan and India, India and China, China and Vietnam). In short, there is no Eurasian power or alliance of Eurasian powers which can at this time effectively counterbalance a revived Heartland power.

Enamored of our victory in the ideological Cold War, many Western observers have failed to appreciate the remarkable coalition and immense effort that effectively contained Soviet Heartland power. Over a forty-five-year period, the United States constructed and anchored an arc of containment stretching from Japan, the Philippines, and Australia in the Pacific, to South Korea, and China in East Asia, to Pakistan, Afghanistan, and the Persian Gulf in Southwest Asia, to Israel, Saudi Arabia, and Egypt in the Middle East, to Central and Western Europe, and to Scandinavia and the North Atlantic. Millions of dollars were spent on European and Japanese recovery from the devastation of World War II. Many billions of dollars more were spent on a huge military establishment, including thousands of nuclear weapons and the most powerful navy in the world. Two lengthy "hot" wars were fought on the Asian mainland, and many smaller conflicts were endured. This monumental effort was required to forestall the third attempt in this century by a Eurasian power to dominate the World-Island.

The geopolitical imperative of preventing a single power or alliance of powers from dominating the Eurasian landmass is as valid today as it was in 1812, 1914, 1940 and 1946. The dramatic events of the past few years in the Heartland have weakened the power that threatened Eurasian hegemony for the last forty-five years. But the balance of power on Eurasia has not altered to such an extent that America's weight can safely be removed from the scales. This is not to say that America's military role in Europe and Asia cannot be reduced, modified or restructured to some extent. However, what America's foremost geopolitical thinker, Nicholas Spykman, wrote in 1942 still holds true today:

> it will be cheaper in the long run to remain a working member of the Eur-[asian] power zone than to withdraw for short intermissions to our insular domain only to be forced to apply later the whole of our national strength to redress a balance that might have needed but a slight weight at the beginning.[34]

"The United States must recognize," counseled Spykman, "that the power constellation in Europe and Asia is of everlasting concern to her, both in time of war and in time of peace."[35]

The new Mr. X, then, should recognize the significant changes that have occurred in the world in recent years, but analyze those changes within the rich tradition of American and Western geopolitical thought. This will necessarily entail a look backward into American history, and, equally important, a look backward into world history. For as Zbigniew Brzezinski pointed out in his masterful geopolitical study, *Game Plan,* the U.S.-Soviet conflict was "the legatee of the old, almost traditional, and certainly geopolitical clash between great oceanic powers and the dominant land powers."[36] The new Mr. X should read Brzezinski and Spykman and Mahan and especially Mackinder. American foreign policy, to be effective in the post-Cold War world, must be based on sound geographical and historical knowledge and understanding.

Notes

1.   George F. Kennan, *American Diplomacy* (Chicago: University of Chicago Press, 1951), p. 99.
2.   Much of Kennan's thought on nuclear war is collected in *The Nuclear Delusion* (New York: Pantheon Books, 1983).
3.   Kennan, *American Diplomacy,* op. cit., p. 105.
4.   See for example, Edward N. Luttwak, "From Geopolitics to Geoeconomics," *National Interest,* Summer 1990, pp. 17-24; Zbigniew Brzezinski, "Beyond Chaos: What the West Must Do," *National Interest,* Spring 1990, pp. 3-12; Irving Kristol, "Defining Our National Interest," *National Interest,* Fall 1990, pp. 16-25; Charles Krauthammer, "Universal Dominion: Toward a Unipolar World," *National Interest,* Winter 1989/90, pp. 46-49; Andrew C. Goldberg, "Challenges to the Post-Cold War Balance of Power," *Washington Quarterly,* Winter 1991, pp. 51-60; Lee Edwards, "Beyond the Cold War," *The World & I,* September 1990, pp. 22-29; Bruce D. Porter, "The Coming Resurgence of Russia," *National Interest,* Spring 1991, pp. 14-23.
5.   However, for an explicit attempt to apply geopolitical principles to the formulation of U.S. strategy and force structure, see Mackubin Thomas Owens, "Force Planning in an Era of Uncertainty," *Strategic Review,* Spring 1990, pp. 9-22.
6.   Quoted in Norman A. Graebner, *Ideas and Diplomacy: Readings in the Intellectual Tradition of American Foreign Policy* (New York: Oxford University Press, 1964), p. 71
7.   *The Federalist,* No. 11.
8.   Quoted in Graebner, op. cit., p. 11.
9.   Ibid., p. 111
10.   Ibid., p. 122.
11.   Ibid., pp. 123-124.
12.   Ibid., p. 79.
13.   Ibid., p. 143.

14. Ibid., p. 224.
15. Ibid., pp. 215-216.
16. Ibid., pp. 252-253.
17. Ibid., p. 218.
18. Halford J. Mackinder, *Democratic Ideals and Reality* (New York: W.W. Norton and Co., 1962), pp. 241-242. This volume contains Mackinder's additional papers that discuss his Heartland theory: "The Geographical Pivot of History" (1904) and "The Round World and the Winning of the Peace" (1443). *Democratic Ideals and Reality* was originally written in 1919.
19. For a more detailed analysis of Mackinder's geopolitical writings, see, Francis P. Sempa. "Geopolitics and American Strategy: A Reassessment," *Strategic Review*, Spring 1987, pp. 27-38. This article was reprinted in Herbert M. Levine and Jean Edward Smith, eds., *The Conduct of American Foreign Policy Debated* (New York: McGraw-Hill Publishing Co., 1990), pp. 330-343.
20. Mackinder's 1943 article, "The Round World and the Winning of the Peace," was originally published in the July 1943 issue of *Foreign Affairs*.
21. Mahan's geopolitical views are most comprehensively set forth in *The Problem of Asia* (Boston: Little Brown and Co., 1900). He is best remembered for his trilogy, *The Influence of Sea Power Upon History*. For exhaustive discussions of Mahan's life and writings, see Robert Seager, *Alfred Thayer Mahan: The Man and His Letters* (Annapolis, MD: Naval Institute Press, 1977) and William E. Livezey, *Mahan on Sea Power* (Norman: University of Oklahoma Press, 1981).
22. Quoted in Graebner, op. cit., pp. 428-434.
23. Ibid., p. 600.
24. Mackinder, in 1919, recommended that some "airy cherub" should whisper to Western statesmen the following saying: "Who rules East Europe commands the Heartland: Who rules the Heartland commands the World-Island: Who rules the World-Island commands the world." See *Democratic Ideals and Reality*, p. 150.
25. Walter Lippmann, *U.S. Foreign Policy: Shield of the Republic* (Boston: Little, Brown and Co., 1943), p. 138.
26. Spykman's two geopolitical masterpieces were *America's Strategy in World Politics* (New York: Harcourt, Brace and Co., 1942) and *The Geography of the Peace* (New York: Harcourt, Brace and Co., 1944).
27. Spykman, *America's Strategy in World Politics*, op. cit., p. 4.
28. Lippmann, op. cit., p. 111.
29. Ibid., p. 94.
30. Ibid., pp. 94-95.
31. Colin S. Gray, *The Geopolitics of Super Power* (Lexington: University Press of Kentucky, 1988), p. 4.
32. See Geoffrey Kemp, "Regional Security, Arms Control, and the End of the Cold War," *Washington Quarterly*, Autumn 1990, pp. 33-51.
33. Mark N. Katz, "Beyond the Reagan Doctrine: Reassessing U.S. Policy Toward Regional Conflicts," *Washington Quarterly*, Winter 1991, pp. 169-179.
34. Spykman, *America's Strategy in World Politics*, op. cit., pp. 467-468.
35. Spykman, *The Geography of the Peace*, op. cit., p. 60.
36. Zbigniew Brzezinski, *Game Plan: How to Conduct the U.S.-Soviet Contest* (Boston: Atlantic Monthly Press, 1986), p. 12.

7

Why Teach Geopolitics

In 1977, the strategic analyst Colin Gray lamented the fact that the great geopolitical authors—such as Halford Mackinder and Nicholas Spykman—had appeared on very few university book lists in the 1970s. Ten years later, in an article in *Strategic Review,* this author noted "the virtual eclipse of geopolitics in the American academic realm beginning in the late 1960's."[1] No single factor was responsible for the decline of geopolitics as a separate and important course of study in our colleges and universities, but two factors appear preeminent: domestic reaction to the war in Southeast Asia and Soviet attainment of strategic nuclear parity with the United States. These two developments led, respectively, to a growing disdain for "power politics" and a preoccupation with the nuclear arms race—attitudes particularly pronounced in academia, whose members played so large a role in protesting our involvement in the Vietnam War in the late 1960s and early 1970s, and in promoting disarmament throughout the 1970s up to the present.

The unfortunate result was that for two decades many of our nation's undergraduates never learned the timeless method of geopolitical analysis that underlies all realistic and sensible foreign policy thinking. For two decades, our schools graduated experts on everything from "peace studies" and "Third World studies" to "arms control," while neglecting to equip our future leaders with the knowledge of fundamental geopolitical realities essential to governing a great power in a dangerous and mostly unfriendly world. In fact, the decline of the West's global power position in the 1970s may be traceable, in part, to that intellectual failure.

The study of geopolitics "directs the student toward the important and enduring, as opposed to the trivial and the transient."[2] Friedrich Ratzel, the great German geographer, held that "great statesmen have

103

never lacked a feeling for geography....When one speaks of a healthy political instinct, one usually means a correct evaluation of the geographic bases of political power."[3] Modern global geopolitical thought dates from the latter years of the nineteenth century and received its first comprehensive exposition in a paper delivered by Halford Mackinder to London's Royal Geographical Society in 1904. The paper was titled "The Geographical Pivot of History," and the author's central thesis was that the geographical realities of the planet presented the opportunity for a sufficiently organized and armed great power to control the world's "pivot region"—the northern-central core of Eurasia and, subsequently, establish a world empire. Though Germany and China were potential contenders for world dominance, Mackinder focused his analysis on Russia and compared its strategic position to that of the Mongol Empire of the thirteenth and fourteenth centuries: "Russia replaces the Mongol Empire. Her pressure on Finland, on Scandinavia, on Poland, on Turkey, on Persia, on India, and on China replaces the centrifugal raids on the steppemen. In the world at large she occupies the central strategical position held by Germany in Europe. She can strike on all sides and be struck from all sides, save the north."[4]

Mackinder expanded on this theory fifteen years later in *Democratic Ideals and Reality* (1919), the most influential geopolitical work ever written. He renamed the world's central strategic location the "Heartland" of Eurasia, and referred to the Eurasian-African landmass as the "World Island." Control of the Heartland and Eastern Europe by a single power, he predicted, could lead to dominance of Eurasia and most of the World Island. And, Mackinder warned, "who rules the World Island commands the World."

Technology and rapid means of transportation—motor cars, railways, airplanes—had, according to Mackinder, altered "the relations of men to the larger geographical realities of the world."[5] The era of dominant sea power was at an end. The British Empire had for centuries maintained its predominance by cautiously avoiding permanent alliances with continental powers—by deliberately positioning itself as the "holder" of the European balance of power. As Sir Eyre Crowe explained in his famous Foreign Office Memorandum in 1907, Britain maintained its security and independence "by throwing her weight now in this scale and now in that, but ever on the side opposed to the political dictatorship of the strongest single State or group at a given time."[6] In other words, as long as the power base of the European Continent remained fragmented, British sea power was secure. Mackinder's point was that geography and technology presented the opportunity for a great land power based in the Heartland to dominate all of Eurasia and utilize the great Continent's vast resources to build a navy that would be second to none.

Mackinder's analysis ran counter in some respects to the historical-theoretical writings of Alfred Thayer Mahan, the American strategist and the most influential proponent of sea power. In three major works—*The Influence of Sea Power Upon History, 1660-1783* (1890), *The Influence of Sea Power Upon the French Revolution and Empire, 1793-1812* (1892), and *Sea Power in Its Relation to the War of 1812* (1905)—and numerous other books and articles, Mahan developed a "philosophy of sea power" which focused on six fundamental national factors: geographical position, physical conformation, extent of territory, population, national character, and governmental institutions. Mahan believed that, with a sufficient land base, sea powers, such as Britain and the US, attained strategic preeminence and could remain preeminent by acquiring secure overseas bases, controlling "narrow seas" (what are now called strategic "chokepoints") and "lines of communication" ("lines of movement between the force and its sources of supply"), and by adhering to the principle of concentration of force in time of war. While recognizing Russia's position as the dominant Eurasian land power, Mahan nevertheless felt that Britain and America could secure world dominance by acquiring and maintaining key land bases surrounding Eurasia.

The two world wars of the twentieth century can be viewed in geopolitical terms as clashes between continental land powers and insular maritime powers for control-denial of the "rimlands" of Eurasia—those states on the outer peninsulas of the Eurasian landmass. Had Germany (under the Kaiser or Hitler) succeeded in uniting under its political control the power centers of the Eurasian Continent, the security and independence of Britain and America would have been gravely imperiled. That point was forcefully argued by the American scholar Nicholas Spykman in his two geopolitical masterpieces: *America's Strategy in World Politics* (1942) and *The Geography of the Peace* (1944). Reflecting on the extent of German-Japanese hegemony in 1942, Spykman warned: "We were then confronted with the possibility of complete encirclement, in which case we might have had to face the unified power of the whole Eurasian landmass. The strength of the power centers of the Eastern Hemisphere would then have been overpowering. It would have been impossible for us to preserve our independence and security."[7] He urged American statesmen to recognize that "the safety and independence of this country can be preserved only by a foreign policy that will make it impossible for the Eurasian landmass to harbor overwhelming dominant power in Europe and the Far East."[8]

After World War II, alliances shifted but the nature of the geopolitical clash remained unaltered: Soviet land power, in control of the Heartland and Eastern Europe, was opposed by the American maritime power allied with the rimland states of Eurasia. Remarkably, Mackinder foresaw this geopolitical power distribution in 1943 when, in an article in *Foreign Affairs,* he included an additional feature in his Heartland concept: the "Midland Ocean," consisting of an alliance between the United States, Canada, and the nations of Western Europe.[9]

The geopolitical theories of Mackinder, Mahan, and Spykman were debated and discussed extensively by prominent observers such as James Burnham, Walter Lippmann, Raymond Aron, Hans Weigert, Robert Strausz-Hupé, Derwent Whittlesey, Richard Hartshorne, Margaret Sprout, Alfred Vagts, Jean Gottman, and George Renner. The American postwar policy of containment, first theorized by George Kennan in the "Long Telegram" from Moscow and the "X" article in *Foreign Affairs,* had an implicit geographical focus—containing Soviet communism within the postwar geographical boundaries. NATO, CENTO, SEATO, and similar alliances were formed with the express purpose of preventing Soviet communist expansion into the Eurasian rimlands.

The 1960s began propitiously for the study of geopolitics: containment was still in vogue, and Professor Saul Cohen in 1963 published *Geography and Politics in a World Divided,* an analysis of prior geopolitical writings and their application to the nuclear age. A year earlier, Norton Company had published a paperback edition of Mackinder's *Democratic Ideals and Reality* which included his 1904 essay, "The Geographical Pivot of History," and his 1943 piece in *Foreign Affairs.* Unfortunately, as the 1960's "progressed" in Washington, strategists were replaced by bureaucratic "managers," as Robert McNamara and his "whiz kids" in the Pentagon sought to "manage" the war in Southeast Asia rather than to win it, and to "manage" or "control" the nuclear arms race rather than to win it.

Intellectually appealing concepts, such as Mutual Assured Destruction (MAD) and Management by Objective (MBO), dominated Washington and spread to academia. As the Vietnam War grew more unpopular on college campuses and in the media, "power politics" and anything associated with it fell into disrepute. The result, as Colin Gray has pointed out, was that "many introductory courses in international relation [began to] treat power politics as a passing phase in the history of academic international relations scholarship."[10] Mackinder and Spykman disappeared from university book lists. This left "the professor of international relations and his unfortunate students. . . rudderless in a highly dangerous world."[11] Without a geopolitical framework, it was easy to dismiss as inconsequential the loss of American bases in South Vietnam; the communization of all of Indochina; Soviet acquisition of Angola, Ethiopia, South Yemen, Mozambique, and Nicaragua; the loss of Iran as a U.S. ally in the Persian Gulf region; and the loss of U.S. nuclear superiority. In the wake of these developments, universities continued to emphasize courses on "peace studies," "women's studies," "human rights," "Afro-Asian studies," and the like.

The situation of the late 1960s and early 1970s in academia and Washington has changed. In the past several years, important books on geopolitics have been written by respected scholars: Zbigniew Brzezinski's *Game Plan* (1986), *The Grand Chessboard* (1997), and *The Geostrategic Triad* (2001), Colin Gray's *The Geopolitics of Superpower* (1988) and *The Leverage of Sea Power* (1992), and Paul Kennedy's *The Rise and Fall of the Great Powers* (1988). Brzezinski and Gray, in particular, present brilliant geopolitical analyses, applying the theories and concepts of Mackinder, Spykman, et al. to contemporary international relations. Their books should accompany historical works in university courses devoted to geopolitics and foreign policy.

As America enters a new century, it faces many urgent and complex problems. With limited resources, extensive commitments, and a changing domestic and international political environment in an era of rapid technological change, the United States must make difficult choices and trade-offs in formulating a global strategy. To approach foreign and defense policy decisions in a piecemeal fashion— in a global strategic vacuum— is to court disaster. If our colleges and universities are true to their purpose, they will reinstitutionalize the teaching of geopolitics and, thereby, prepare our future leaders to govern this nation prudently into the twenty-first century and beyond.

Notes

1. Francis P. Sempa, "Geopolitics and American Strategy: A Reassessment," *Strategic Review*, Spring 1987, p.33.
2. Gray, *The Geopolitics of the Nuclear Era* (New York: Crane, Russak, 1977), p. 2.
3. Quoted in Nicholas Spykman, *America 's Strategy in World Politics* (New York: Harcourt, Brace, 1942), p. 165.
4. Halford Mackinder, *Democratic Ideals and Reality* (New York: Norton, 1962), p. 262.
5. Ibid., p. 74.
6. "Foreign Office Memorandum on the Present State of British Relations with France and Germany, January 1, 1907," *British Documents on the Origins of War, 1898-1914*, Volume 3, pp. 402-403.
7. Nicholas Spykman, *The Geography of the Peace* (New York: Harcourt, Brace, 1944), p. 34.
8. Ibid., p. 60.
9. Mackinder, "The Round World and the Winning of the Peace," *Foreign Affairs*, July 1943.
10. Gray, loc cit.
11. Ibid., p.4.

8

Geopolitics in the Twenty-First Century

The brilliant geopolitical thinker and strategist James Burnham began his book, *Suicide of the West*, by reflecting on the immense value of an historical atlas to his craft. "Leafing through an historical atlas," he explained, "we see history as if through a multiple polarizing glass that reduces the infinite human variety to a single rigorous dimension: effective political control over acreage."[1] Geopolitics is very much about "effective political control over acreage." International politics takes place within a geographic context. Nation-states and empires occupy specific geographic areas that we call countries, and they interact with other nation-states or empires within geographic regions, all of which are located on the same globe.

Throughout much of recorded history, the earth was not what Halford Mackinder called a "closed political system." Political events in one part or region of the globe did not necessarily affect any other part or region. For example, the Roman Empire controlled much of Western Europe, the Mediterranean Sea, parts of the Middle East and North Africa, but it had little impact on the Chinese Empire of that time period. That changed toward the end of what Mackinder called "the Columbian epoch," and what others have called the "age of discovery." Prior to the "Columbian epoch," geopolitics was regional. Gradually, as more and more of the globe fell under the political sway of European and Asian powers, the field of geopolitics expanded. By the beginning of the twentieth century, the geographic context of international politics was the entire globe.

My historical atlas begins in 1400 B.C. and shows the Hittite, Mitanni, and Egyptian Empires grouped around the Eastern Mediterranean, with the Kassites in control of the region where the Tigris and Euphrates Rivers flow into the Persian Gulf. The next map shows the same areas in the seventh century B.C. dominated by the Assyrian

Empire. Three hundred years later, a map of the same area shows the region dominated by the Persian Empire and notes the rise of the Greek city-states. By the third century B.C., Alexander the Great's Empire dominates the region. The next two maps show the rise of the Roman Empire which at its height in 120 A.D. controlled all the land surrounding the Mediterranean Sea and England. Three hundred years later, the map of Europe shows the invasion routes of the Huns, Visigoths, Vandals, Franks, Lombards, Ostrogoths, Burgundians, and Anglo-Saxons. In Asia during this time period, India is controlled by the Mauryans and Guptas, while China is ruled by the Han, T'ang and Sung dynasties. Meanwhile, the Yamoto's gained control of Japan and began to develop an independent state. In the 800s, the map shows Charlemagne's Empire stretching from the Pyrenees to modern Germany. In the twelfth century, Europe begins to take shape: Poland, Hungary, the Holy Roman Empire, France, and England are independent states or kingdoms. Moslem sultanates and caliphates control the Middle East and North Africa. Spain is divided into separate kingdoms, while Kievan Rus begins to expand in Eastern Europe.

In the thirteenth century, the maps of Europe and Asia reveal the Mongol explosion from the inner recesses of Asia. At its height, Mongol rule extended from Siberia, Korea, and China to Eastern Europe and Persia. For the first time, the seemingly separate civilizations of Europe and East Asia were significantly affected by a single geopolitical event. The decline of the Mongol Empire two centuries later roughly coincided with the beginning of the "Columbian epoch" or "age of discovery."

For the next four centuries, Dutch, English, French, Italian, Russian, Portuguese, and Spanish explorers gradually filled in the remaining blanks on the world map. Meanwhile, on the Eurasian continent beginning in the sixteenth century, a series of empires threatened to upset the balance of power: the Hapsburgs under Charles V and Phillip II; France under Louis XIV and Napoleon Bonaparte; Germany under Kaiser Wilhelm II and Hitler; and the Soviet Union. In each instance, a coalition of powers, eventually led by Great Britain and the United States, successfully opposed the bid for hegemony.

A key date in the geopolitics of history is 1740. That year saw the beginning of a "trilogy of wars" known to history as the War of Austrian Succession, the Seven Years' War, and the War of American Independence, conflicts during which the European struggle for power spread to much of the rest of the world.[2] From that time forward, every major European war had global repercussions. The era of regional geopolitics was over.

The global conflicts of the eighteenth, nineteenth and twentieth centuries involved repeated, though not exclusive, clashes between land powers and maritime powers. This is a recurring theme in the literature of geopolitics. Geography conditions the land or sea orientation of countries. Island nations, such as Great Britain and Japan, are natural maritime powers. The United States, free from land challenges on the North American continent throughout most of its history, is also a maritime power. On the other hand, countries that are essentially landlocked, such as Russia and Germany, tend to be land powers. Finally, there are countries like France, India, and China that are primarily land powers but have ready access to the ocean.

Since 1740 the maritime powers have fared rather well in international politics. First Great Britain, then the United States, was able to organize and underwrite global coalitions to defeat challenges from great land powers (France, Germany, and the Soviet Union). Colin S. Gray, in *The Leverage of Sea Power*, contends that "[g]reat sea powers or maritime coalitions have either won or, occasionally drawn every major war in modern history."[3] But, as Gray acknowledges, maritime powers often succeeded in those instances by forming alliances with other land powers, and often by using sea power to directly intervene in land struggles. It was never purely a sea power versus land power struggle. Contrary to popular belief, the worldviews of Mackinder and the American naval historian Alfred Thayer Mahan are not diametric opposites. Both recognized the immense value of sea power in a world where three-quarters of the earth's surface is water. Both believed that all other things being equal an insular geographical position was the most favorable position. Finally, both believed that the continent of Eurasia was the principal arena of struggle for the great powers.

That brings us to another recurring theme in the literature of geopolitics: the centrality of Eurasia. Most of the key events of world history occurred on the Eurasian landmass or one of its offshore islands. Much of the rest of the world at one time or another became the object of expansion, settlement and colonization by one or more Eurasian or offshore Eurasian powers. Mackinder called Eurasia "the Great Continent." Brzezinski calls it "the mega-continent." Eurasia is the globe's largest landmass and contains most of the world's people and resources. Fortunately, the geopolitical region of Eurasia and its offshore islands has throughout history remained politically divided. Geopoliticians from Mackinder to Brzezinski repeatedly have stressed the importance of preventing a single power or alliance of powers from controlling the major power centers of Eurasia. The Mongol Empire at its height, Nazi Germany-controlled Europe in alliance with the Soviet Union and Japan in 1940, and the Sino-Soviet bloc in the early 1950s came the nearest to achieving hegemony in Eurasia.

The defeat of the Soviet Union by a maritime coalition led by the United States ended the most recent bid for global hegemony by a great Eurasian-based land power. The end of the Cold War and the emergence of the "information revolution" produced several articles and books that consigned "geopolitics" to the ash heap of history. The fulcrum of international politics, we were told, would be "globalization" (Thomas Friedman), the microchip (George Gilder) or "geo-economics" (Edward Luttwak). The traditional elements of a nation's power—geographical position, military power, character of government, population, industrial and economic power—would be replaced by trade relations, environmental cooperation and global information networks. An increasingly interdependent world, it was argued, would be less prone to military and political conflicts. International relations would no longer be an arena dominated by "power politics" and the struggle for territory.

Yet, the Cold War was barely over when Saddam Hussein's Iraq attempted to forcibly seize the oil wealth of the Middle East by conquering Kuwait and threatening Saudi Arabia. That was followed by Russia's war against Chechen separatists, the Serbs' attempt to dominate the former Yugoslavia, North Korea's development and testing of ballistic missiles, China's efforts to intimidate Taiwan and assert control over the South China Sea, a revival of the Israeli-Palestinian conflict and nuclear jousting by India and Pakistan over disputed territory in Kashmir. The central importance of geopolitics reasserted itself. Events proved that geography and spatial power relationships still mattered.

This did not go unrecognized in the scholarly community. In the Spring 1996 issue of *Orbis*, Colin S. Gray observed that "world politics is still keyed to territorially based and defined states." "[T]hough the geographical setting does not determine the course of history," he wrote, "it is fundamental to all that happens within its boundaries." Gray concluded that "geographical factors are pervasive in world politics." "Geography," he explained, "defines the players (which are territorially organized states, or would like to be), frequently defines the stakes for which the players contend, and always defines the terms in which they measure their security one to the other."[4] In a more recent article in the *Journal of Strategic Studies*, Gray writes that "all political matters...have a geopolitical dimension," and concludes that for the study and practice of international relations "geography is inescapable."[5]

Former National Security Adviser Zbigniew Brzezinski weighed in on the subject in 1997 with his book, *The Grand Chessboard*. Brzezinski identified the "megacontinent" of Eurasia as the geopolitical stage on which the great powers will vie for predominance in the future. A stable global balance of power, he explained, requires "geopolitical pluralism" on the Eurasian continent. "Competition based on territory," he wrote, " still dominates world affairs." In Brzezinski's world-view, "geographic location is still the point of departure for the definition of a nation-state's external priorities, and the size of national territory also remains one of the major criteria of status and power." In his latest work, *The Geostrategic Triad*, Brzezinski explores the current and future geopolitical interaction of the United States with Europe, Russia and China.[6]

In 1999, Boston College's Robert S. Ross, in an article the title of which was borrowed from one of Nicholas Spykman's seminal books on geopolitics, explored the emerging geopolitical struggle in East Asia. Ross, like Gray and Brzezinski, emphasized the importance of geography. "Although many factors contribute to great power status, including economic development and levels of technology and education," he wrote, " geography determines whether a country has the prerequisites of great power status; it determines which states *can* be great powers." Ross' article focused on what he called "the geography of the twenty-first-century balance of power."[7]

Perhaps the most explicit argument for the continuing relevance of geopolitics to the study and practice of international relations is found in Mackubin Thomas Owens' article, "In Defense of Classical Geopolitics," which appeared in the Autumn 1999 issue of the *Naval War College Review*. In the article, Owens directly rebuts the "end of history," "globalization," and "geo-economic" schools of thought. "Real international relations," he writes, "occur in real geographic space." "[A]ll international politics…takes place in time and space, in particular geographical settings and environments." "Geography," explains Owens, "defines limits and opportunities in international politics."[8]

The editors of the *Journal of Strategic Studies* recently devoted a special issue to the topic of "Geopolitics, Geography and Strategy," which includes an article by Jon Sumida on the continuing relevance of some of the geopolitical ideas of Mahan, and a piece by Geoffrey Sloan on Mackinder. Sumida writes that some of Mahan's concerns "have remained central issues for current students of geopolitics." Sloan contends that "Mackinder through the heartland theory has left a theoretical legacy which can be utilized to outline the geographical perspective of the twenty-first century."[9]

What is the "geopolitical perspective" of this new century? In broad terms, using traditional geopolitical concepts, the emerging global power structure resembles the Mackinder-Spykman framework. Most of the Eurasian heartland is controlled by a weakened, but still potentially powerful Russia. The Eurasian rimland is divided into geopolitical regions: Europe, the Middle East, Southwest Asia and East Asia-Pacific Rim.

The United States dominates the Western Hemisphere and participates in the power balance in every region of the Eurasian rimland. Whereas Great Britain once was the "holder" of the European balance of power, the United States is today the "holder" of the world balance of power. The United States is the only country capable of using its power to influence events in every part of the world.

The "great continent" of Eurasia, however, remains what Brzezinski calls "the grand chessboard" of world politics. The power potential of Eurasia still dwarfs that of any other region of the globe. Just consider the consequences for the rest of the world if one power or an alliance of powers had control over the combined human, natural, scientific, and technological resources of Europe, Russia, the Middle East, Southwest Asia (India and its neighbors), East Asia and the Pacific Rim (including China and Japan), or even a considerable portion of those resources. Mackinder's nightmarish vision of a world empire would be in sight.

At the dawn of this new century there is no country or alliance of countries that currently threatens to upset what Brzezinski calls the "geopolitical pluralism" of Eurasia. The United States continues to exert its influence onto the rimland of Eurasia via alliances or strategic partnerships with rimland countries (NATO, Israel, Saudi Arabia, Egypt, Japan, South Korea, Australia, etc.), pre-positioning of military power in those regions, and its unequalled sea and air power. But the current geopolitical equilibrium will not last forever. The future of NATO is uncertain. The European Union is beginning to emerge as an independent (from the United States) power center. The future alignment of Ukraine, the newly independent states of Central Asia, some of the former Warsaw Pact countries and the Baltic Republics is still in doubt. Russia will not be prostrate forever, and it still occupies most of the "heartland" of Eurasia. India's population and military power, including nuclear power, continue to grow. Japan, though currently in an economic slump, has enormous economic power that it could translate into military power. Meanwhile, China possesses the geographic location, the human and natural resources, and the will to bid for predominance in the East Asia-Pacific Rim region and, perhaps, beyond.

In geopolitical terms, the U.S.-Chinese relationship in the East Asia-Pacific Rim region is a rivalry between a maritime superpower with global interests and responsibilities and a dominant regional land power with superpower ambitions and access to the ocean. Even if China's ambitions are limited to regional hegemony, competition with the United States is inevitable. A U.S. forward presence in Japan, on the Korean peninsula and elsewhere in East Asia and the Pacific Rim is, in the long term, incompatible with Chinese regional hegemony.

It can, therefore, be expected that China will pursue policies designed to expel the United States from its influential role in the region. This may take many forms. Diplomatically, China may seek to undermine U.S. alliances with Japan and South Korea, while simultaneously improving its own relations with Russia and India. Militarily, China may take steps, such as continued pressure on Taiwan and elsewhere in the South China Sea, to expose U.S. military and political commitments as unreliable. Strategically, China may challenge the United States' superiority in sea, air and space power (for example, by building and/or buying more warships, jet fighters and bombers, and intercontinental ballistic missiles armed with weapons of mass destruction). During the recent crisis in the Taiwan Strait, a Chinese official publicly questioned whether the United States would be willing to sacrifice Los Angeles to prevent China's conquest of Taiwan—a not so subtle reminder that China may believe that it may soon be able to deter the United States from interfering with China's goals in the region.

In the 1830s, a wise Frenchman named Alexis De Tocqueville accurately predicted a future global rivalry between Russia and the United States. A few decades before that, another wise Frenchman, Napoleon Bonaparte, called China the "sleeping giant," and advised the world's statesmen to let her sleep because when she wakes she "will move the world." China has awaken from her centuries long sleep to take her place among the world's great powers in the twenty-first century. How the world's other powers, particularly the United States, react to China's rise will likely dominate the geopolitics of the twenty-first century.

Geopolitics in the twenty-first century will also be affected by the ongoing struggle for control of outer space. We are beginning to see articles and books that discuss "astropolitics" as an extension of traditional geopolitics. For example, Everett C. Dolman has presented an "astropolitical" analysis of world politics that relies considerably on the ideas and concepts of Mackinder and Mahan.[10] Space power enthusiasts, however, should avoid the temptation to oversell the strategic value of space power the way the early air power enthusiasts oversold air power's capabilities.

At the end of the Cold War, President George H.W. Bush proclaimed a "new world order," just as his predecessors, Woodrow Wilson and Franklin Roosevelt, envisioned new world orders (the League of Nations and United Nations) following the twentieth century's two previous global conflicts. All three presidents were wrong because in their desire to bestow upon their citizens a permanently peaceful world they ignored the enduring geopolitical realities of our earthly home.

Notes

1.   James Burnham, *Suicide of the West: An Essay on the Meaning and Destiny of Liberalism* (Chicago: Regnery Books, 1985), p. 14. The book was originally published in 1964.
2.   This is one of the themes of R.J. Seeley's brilliant work, *The Expansion of England* (Boston: Little Brown and Company, 1901).
3.   Colin S. Gray, *The Leverage of Sea Power: The Strategic Advantage of Navies in War* (New York: The Free Press, 1992), p. ix.
4.   Colin S. Gray, "How Geopolitics Influences Security," *Orbis* (Spring 1996), p. 2.
5.   Colin S. Gray, "Inescapable Geography," *Journal of Strategic Studies* (June/September 1999), pp. 164-165.

6.   Zbigniew Brzezinski, *The Grand Chessboard: American Primacy and its Geostrategic Imperatives* (New York: Basic Books, 1997), p. 38; Zbigniew Brzezinski, *The Geostrategic Triad* (Washington, DC: Center for Strategic and International Studies, 2001).
7.   Robert S. Ross, "The Geography of the Peace: East Asia in the Twenty-first Century," *International_Security* (Spring 1999), pp. 81-82.
8.   Mackubin Thomas Owens, "In Defense of Classical Geopolitics," *Naval War College Review* (Autumn 1999), www.nwc.navy.mil/press/review/1999/autumn/art3-a99.htm.
9.   Jon Sumida, "Alfred Thayer Mahan, Geopolitician," *The Journal of Strategic Studies* (June/September 1999), p.59; Geoffrey Sloan, "Sir Halford Mackinder: The Heartland Theory Then and Now," *Journal of Strategic Studies* (June/September 1999), p. 35.
10.   Everett C. Dolman, "Geostrategy in the Space Age: An Astropolitical Analysis," *Journal of Strategic_Studies* (June/September, 1999), pp. 83-106. Dolman has expanded his article into a book entitled *Astropolitik: Classical Geopolitics in the Space Age* (London: Frank Cass Publishers, 2001).

Index

Adams, John, 89
Adams, Thomas B., 90
Aden, 55
Adriatic Sea, 17
Afghanistan, 78, 99
Africa, 5, 14, 19, 28, 67, 69, 83, 91
Air War College, 55
Alaska, 19
Alexander the Great, 110
Algeria, 55
Allen, William, 90
American Committee for Cultural Freedom, 54
American Geographical Society, 21
American Mercury, 53
American Workers Party, 40, 41
America's Strategy in World Politics, 75, 105
Amery, Leo, 34
Anglo-Saxons, 110
Angola, 77, 107
Anti-satellite weapon, 4
Aral Sea, 16
Arctic Ocean, 16, 26, 92
Argentina, 5, 98
Armenia, 70
Armstrong, Hamilton F., 18
Aron, Raymond, 34, 72, 106
Assyrian Empire, 109-110
Athens, 69
Atlantic Monthly, 54
Atlantic Ocean, 6, 33, 91, 92, 97
Australia, 5, 12, 14, 26, 91, 99
Austria (Austria-Hungary), 4, 12, 48, 49
Avars, 12, 27, 29, 68

Balance of power, 4, 6, 11, 25, 34, 42, 74, 75, 88-90, 93, 104, 114
Ballistic missile defenses, 4
Baltic Sea, 17, 18, 19, 70
Baluchistan, 16, 69

Barnes, Harry E., 53
Barrett, William, 41, 46
Belgium, 7
Belorussia, 96
Bentley, Elizabeth, 54-55
Berle, Adolf, 40
Berlin, 49, 55
Berlin Wall, 59, 60
Bismarck, Otto von, 30
Black Sea, 17, 18, 70
Blouet, Brian, 9
Bolsheviks, 13
Brazil, 5, 98
Britain and the British Seas, 10-11
Brzezinski, Zbigniew, 20, 100, 107, 111-114
Buchanan, Patrick, 97
Buckley, William F., 55
Bulgarians, 12, 27
Burgundians, 110
Burnham, Claude, 39
Burnham, James, 3, 7, 34, 39-63, 73-74, 77, 84, 106, 109, Trotskyist, 40-41; Stalinism, 42-43, 46; "Sixth Turn of the Communist Screw", 45; containment, 49-50, 73; Truman, 51; liberation, 51-52, 73; Mackinder, 52; McCarthyism, 54; *National Review*, 55-58;
Vietnam War, 57-58; Sino-Soviet split, 56; Cuban missile crisis, 56; missile defense, 57; Panama Canal, 57; détente, 58; liberalism, 59-60; Medal of Freedom, 60; death of, 60; "zone of war vs. zone of peace", 74
Busch, Andrew, 59
Bush, George H.W., 116

Camp David Accord, 60
Canada, 12, 19, 33, 72
Caribbean Sea, 19, 67

119

Hamilton, Alexander, 55, 89
Hapsburgs, 4, 110
Hardman, J.B.S., 40
Hartshorne, Richard, 106
Harvard University, 10
Haushofer, Karl, 17, 18, 32, 71
Heartland, 11, 15-21, 29-31, 33, 35, 45-48, 50, 52, 69-73, 78, 80, 82-83, 92, 95, 98-99, 104, 106, 114, 115
Hess Rudolf, 18, 32
Hill, Emily, 20
History of the Russian Revolution, 40
Hitchens, Christopher, 44
Hitler, Adolf, 4, 18, 31-33, 42, 44, 71, 105, 110
Hittite Empire, 109
Hobbes, Thomas, 55
Holy Roman Empire, 110
Hook, Sidney, 40
House of Commons, 13
Humboldt, Alexander von, 32
Hungary, 110
Huns, 12, 16, 27, 29, 68, 110
Hussein, Saddam, 112

India, 4, 12, 15, 19, 27, 68, 98-99, 104, 110-112, 114-115
Indian Ocean, 97
Indochina, 50, 55
Industrial revolution, 27
Introduction to Philosophical Analysis, 40
Iran, 4, 49, 77, 98, 107
Iraq, 98, 112
Israel, 56, 98, 99
Italy, 48, 49

Japan, 4, 5, 12-13, 18, 26, 35, 42, 44, 68, 76, 83, 88, 91, 97, 99, 110, 112, 114-115
Jefferson, Thomas, 55, 90, 93-95
Johns Hopkins University, 43
Johnson, Lyndon, 57
Judis, John, 43

Kalmuks, 12, 27, 68
Kampuchea, 77
Kant, Immanuel, 32, 55
Kassites, 109
Kazakhstan, 96
Kennan, George F., 25, 26, 39, 45, 48, 52-53, 56, 67-68, 87-88, 94-95, 106

Kennedy, John F., 57
Kennedy, Paul, 20, 107
Khazars, 12, 27, 68
Kirkpatrick, Jeane, 58
Kissinger, Henry, 6, 20, 58
Kjellen, Rudolf, 18, 32, 71
Korea, 4, 12, 15, 25, 48-50, 83, 97-99, 110, 112, 115
Korean War, 25, 77
Kristol, Irving, 82
Kurile Islands, 48, 49

League of Nations, 17, 71, 116
Lena River, 16, 33
Lenin, Vladimir, 40, 46
Leverage of Seapower, The, 107, 111
Libya, 98
Liddell Hart, Basil, 55
Life, 18, 53
Lincoln, Abraham, 55
Lippmann, Walter, 34, 72, 93, 94, 106
Lombards, 110
London School of Economics, 13
Lord Curzon, 13
Louis XIV, 4, 110
Luce, Henry, 53
Luttwak, Edward, 3, 112

Macedonia, 69
Machiavelli, Niccolo, 43
Machiavellians, The, 43
Mackinder, Halford, 3, 7, 9-37, 45, 47, 50, 52, 55, 68-73, 76-78, 81, 83-84, 91-93, 100, 103-105, 106, 107, 109, 111-112, 114, 116; early life and education, 9-10; *Britain and the British Seas*, 10-11; pivot paper, 11-13, 26-27, 68, 91, 104; political career, 13-14, 31; *Democratic Ideals and Reality*, 14-17, 28-31, 69-71, 91-92, 104-105; influence on Germany, 18, 32; *Foreign Affairs* article, 18-19, 33, 72; and Mahan, 27, 92, 105; criticism of, 34; influence on Burnham, 45, 47, 50, 52, 73
Madison, James, 55, 94
Magyars, 12, 27, 29, 68
Mahan, Alfred Thayer, 3, 4, 7, 27, 55, 79, 92-95, 100, 105-106, 111, 114, 116
Management by Objective, 107
Managerial Revolution, The, 41-42, 46, 48, 54

Venona, 55
Versailles, 17, 31
Vietnam, 25, 57-58, 99
Vietnam War, 57-58, 77, 103, 107
Visigoths, 110
Volga River, 16

War of 1812, 89
War of American Independence, 110-111
War of the Austrian Succession, 110
Warsaw Pact, 80, 115
War We Are In, The, 44
Walters, R.E., 20
Weapons of mass destruction, 88, 98
Web of Subversion, The, 55
Weigert, Hans, 34, 106
Wheelwright, Phillip, 40
Whittlesey, Derwent, 106

Wilhelm II, 4, 5, 33, 69, 105, 110
Wilson, Woodrow, 81, 116
Winant, John, 21
Winik, Jay, 59
Woerner, Manfred, 80
World-Island, 14-17, 29, 31, 47, 50, 69, 70, 78, 83, 91-93, 94, 104
World War I, 6, 14-17, 20, 27, 30-32, 69, 71, 81
World War II, 13, 18-20, 25, 31, 44-45, 49, 67, 81, 88, 93-94, 99, 106

Yale University, 72
Yalta Conference, 44
Yamotos, 110
Yeltsin, Boris, 88, 95, 96
Yemen, 98, 107
Yenisei River, 16, 19
Yugoslavia, 25, 49, 112